W9-AYB-737

风向标
Wind Vane

Ace the New SAT Verbal Section!

SAT
400必备词汇

Denise Pivarnik-Nova（美）编著 　胡 毅 冯宇则 译

McGraw-Hill's

400 *ESSENTIAL*
SAT
WORDS

外语教学与研究出版社
FOREIGN LANGUAGE TEACHING AND RESEARCH PRESS
北京 BEIJING

京权图字：01－2009－0744

Denise Pivarnik-Nova
400 Essential SAT Words
ISBN: 978-0-07-143494-2
Copyright © 2004 by Denise Pivarnik-Nova.

All Rights reserved. No part of this publication may be reproduced or transmitted in any form or by any means, electronic or mechanical, including without limitation photocopying, recording, taping, or any database, information or retrieval system, without the prior written permission of the publisher.

This authorized Bilingual edition is jointly published by McGraw-Hill Education（Asia）and Foreign Language Teaching and Research Press. This edition is authorized for sale in the People's Republic of China only, excluding Hong Kong SAR, Macao SAR and Taiwan.

Copyright © 2009 by McGraw-Hill Education（Asia）, a division of the Singapore Branch of The McGraw-Hill Companies, Inc. and Foreign Language Teaching and Research Press.

版权所有。未经出版人事先书面许可，对本出版物的任何部分不得以任何方式或途径复制或传播，包括但不限于复印、录制、录音，或通过任何数据库、信息或可检索的系统。

本授权双语版由麦格劳-希尔（亚洲）教育出版公司和外语教学与研究出版社合作出版。此版本经授权仅限在中华人民共和国境内（不包括香港特别行政区、澳门特别行政区和台湾省）销售。

版权 © 2009 由麦格劳-希尔（亚洲）教育出版公司与外语教学与研究出版社所有。

本书封面贴有McGraw-Hill公司防伪标签，无标签者不得销售。

图书在版编目(CIP)数据

SAT400 必备词汇 = 400 Essential SAT Words / （美）皮瓦尼克-诺瓦 (Pivarnik-Nova, D.)编著；胡毅，冯宇则译 . — 北京：外语教学与研究出版社，2009.10

ISBN 978 - 7 -5600 -9101 -3

Ⅰ. S… Ⅱ. ①皮… ②胡… ③冯… Ⅲ. 英语—词汇—高等学校—入学考试—美国—自学参考资料 Ⅳ. H313

中国版本图书馆 CIP 数据核字 (2009) 第 192710 号

你有你"优"——点击你的外语学习方案
www.2u4u.com.cn
阅读、视听、测试、交流
购书享积分，积分换好书

出 版 人：于春迟
责任编辑：刘为华
封面设计：刘 冬
版式设计：蔡 颖
出版发行：外语教学与研究出版社
社　　址：北京市西三环北路 19 号 (100089)
网　　址：http://www.fltrp.com
印　　刷：中国农业出版社印刷厂
开　　本：889×1194　1/32
印　　张：7.375
版　　次：2009 年 11 月第 1 版　2009 年 11 月第 1 次印刷
书　　号：ISBN 978 - 7 -5600 -9101 -3
定　　价：25.00 元（含 MP3 光盘 1 张）
＊　　　＊　　　＊
如有印刷、装订质量问题出版社负责调换
制售盗版必究　举报查实奖励
版权保护办公室举报电话：(010)88817519
物料号：191010001

CONTENTS
目 录

SECTION III

Introduction
引 言

你正在备考新的SAT I吧。这很好。本书将介绍许多你很可能会在SAT I中遇到的单词。新的SAT I不再像以前那样有单独的词汇部分了，而是将词汇纳入到阅读理解部分中。事实上，连学生为之奋斗了多年的类比题也取消了。需要考查的单词融进了阅读的篇章和完成句子题中。这就要求你知道在特定语境中应该使用哪个词。因此，你很需要这本书。它不仅会讲解单词及其含义，而且每一部分的末尾还会有完成句子题和根据故事语境填词的练习。不仅如此，本书还包括三个综合性练习，需要你同时回忆起几个部分中讲授的词汇。虽然SAT I不是一个简单的测试，但只要你努力学习，就可以取得很好的成绩。那么，我们就开始吧。

SAT I
Test-Taking Tips
应试技巧

一、当错误信息即是正确答案时

在多项选择题中，有时候你需要回答这样一个问题："All the following items are present except…"，这时候你需要在五个给出的回答中找出哪一个是在你所阅读的内容中没有出现的。

这样的问题有时候很刁钻。在整个学习生涯中，你都被要求找出正确答案，一般来说也就是要找出那个正确的信息点。而现在，突然要求你找出不正确的那一个，而这个不正确的信息点恰好是正确答案！真的很困难！

不仅如此，这些问题还很费时间。在回答这样的问题时，你不再是只寻找一个信息点，而是必须在发现那个不正确的答案之前，有条不紊地找出四个正确的（或者出现过的）信息点。

做好这类问题最好的办法就是练习、练习、再练习。另外，你也可以先浏览一下五个选项，然后再迅速浏览一遍需要考虑的信息，每发现一个信息就勾出来一个。

的确，这类多选题需要你锻炼脑子。在做完大量的 SAT 模拟试题之后，你做这一类题就得心应手了，而且你会发现，与以前不知道该找什么样信息的时候相比，现在你做这类题所花的时间会少很多。

二、写作和批判性阅读

新 SAT 考试不再有单独的"词汇"部分。测试的英文部分现在被拆分为两个部分：写作和批判性阅读。

写作部分包括找出句子中的错误，润色句子和段落，以及在 25 分钟内根据提示完成一篇短文。

判断性阅读部分包含阅读篇章并回答问题，以及和以前类似的完成句子（词汇）题。所阅读的篇章除小说外，还包括从人文科学、社会研究、自然科学选来的非小说类篇章。此外，新 SAT 的阅读部分新增了简短的篇章，每段只有 100 多个词，之后会有和长篇阅读类似的一到两个问题。考试中也可能会出现总长 200 词左右的两段文字，要求考生根据这两篇文章的内容及它们之间的关系回答四个问题。

三、前缀和后缀

前缀是一组位于单词词首并且影响单词意思的字母(称为词缀)。以单词 able 为例，其意思是"有能力的，胜任的"。如果在它前面加上前缀 un-，构成新词 unable，意思就是"没能力的，不胜任的"。如果将前缀 dis- 置于 able 前面，构成新词 disable，意思就是"使……无法使用"，例如，一辆发动机熄火了的汽车就是一辆无法使用的（disabled）车。

前缀有成百上千个，你不需要知道所有的前缀。但有些你必须记住，它们暗示着单词的意思。前缀 ir-、il-、im-、in-、un- 和 dis- 都表示否定或者相反的意思。前缀 co-、con- 和 com- 的意思都是"与"或者"与……协力"。其他前缀还有 auto-、dis-、bi-、tri-、anti- 和 inter- 等。

一旦意识到这些前缀的存在，并且记住最常用的前缀，那你会在遇到新单词时多一条线索。也许你并不知道 discompose 的确切含义，但你知道如果用 composed 来形容一个人了，他或她做事就很沉着。因此，discomposed 的意思就是"焦虑不安的，心慌意乱的"。

后缀位于一个单词的末尾，可以改变原词词义和词性。诸如 -ness 和 -ability 一类的词尾可以将形容词变成名词。例如，形容词 noble 加上后缀 -ness 后就变成了名词 nobleness，意思是"高尚，崇高"。如果加上后缀 -ability，那么就造出了名词 nobility，意思是"高贵"，有时候也指"贵族"或者"上层阶级"。

另一方面，后缀 -ly 几乎永远都是副词的标志：nobly 的意思是"高尚地，崇高地"。副词总是回答"如何"、"什么时候"、"为什么"、"到什么程度"、"多长时间一次"或者"多少"这样的问题。换句话说：The young princess behaved **nobly** when she visited the orphanage. 这句话告诉了我们她的举止表现。

　　另一个常见的后缀是 -ology，它的意思是"关于……的研究"。例如，biology 就是关于生物或者生命形式的研究，endocrinology 是对内分泌系统的研究。

　　和前缀一样，你需要了解最常用的后缀。尽管后缀可能并不能告诉你单词的意思，但它会帮助你判断单词的用法。有时候知道单词的用法是理解词义的关键一步。

四、评分标准

　　你肯定不想在 SAT 考试中盲目猜测。如果在多选题中你连两个选项都排除不了，你一定无从猜测答案。在 SAT 考试中你的分数取决于你答对的题数。不作答不得分，选错答案则要扣去 0.25 分。

　　也就是说，如果你有 10 个问题，你有 4 题没有回答，那你会得到 6 分。但如果你 10 道题都做了，可是其中 4 题答错了，那么你只能得到 5 分。因此在你猜测并填入答案之前，一定要足够确信这个答案是正确的，其他若干选项都是错误的。

五、了解词性的重要性

　　在你试图找出哪个单词或者词组是完成句子题最合适的答案时，判断出生词是名词、动词、形容词还是副词有时候是很有用的。

　　名词是一个人、一个地点或者一件物品的称谓。要检验一个单词是否是名词形式，你可以在它前面加一个 a、an 或者 the。以 defiance 为例：The **defiance** of the prisoner tried the patience of his lawyer.

　　动词是表示动作或者存在状态的词。在 SAT I 的词汇部分里，动词与动作有关，即使是表示精神上的动作的词也是这样，例如：to think, to study, 又如：The prisoner **defied** the rules of the prison, so he lost all his privileges.

　　形容词修饰名词或者代词。它们是描写性的。例如：The **defiant** prisoner had to be placed in solitary confinement because he would not follow the prison rules.

　　副词修饰动词、形容词或者其他副词。它们常以 -ly 结尾。例如：The prisoner **defiantly** refused to speak to his lawyer. （defiantly 修饰动词，说明 his lawyer 是如何被拒绝的。）The **defiantly** rude prisoner had to find a new defense lawyer. （defiantly 修饰形容词 rude，表示粗鲁的程度。）

SECTION I

Unit 1 Reality or Illusion 现实还是幻想 ►actuality, applicable, authenticity, bona fide, categorical, defensible, factual, genuine, invulnerable, legitimacy, materiality, pragmatic, real McCoy, tangible, tenable, truism, unassailable, valid, veracity, veritable ►aberration, artifice, chimera, deceptive, ephemeral, erroneous, evanescent, fallacy, fantasy, fleeting, hallucination, illusion, imaginative, imprecise, inaccurate, mirage, phantasm, semblance, short-lived, transient, whimsy

Unit 2 How Often? 有多经常？►contingent, episodic, incidental, intermittent, interrupt, oscillate, periodic, recurrent, spasmodic, sporadic, transitory, vacillate ►chronic, coherent, habitual, incessant, indefatigable, insistent, inveterate, perpetual, persevering, persistent, resistant, unremitting

Unit 3 In Order of Importance 按照重要性排序 ►extraneous, immaterial, impalpable, incidental, inconsequential, insubstantial, irrelevant, jot, modicum, nonessential, subordinate, subsidiary, whit ►abstruse, considerable, estimable, intense, momentous, noteworthy, poignant, portend, portentous, profound, rarefied, significant, substantial

Unit 4 Crystal Clear and Sure or Shadowy, Uncertain, and Disturbed 非常清楚的和确定的，难以捉摸的、不确定的和不安的 ►apparent, arrant, clarity, conspicuous, discernible, distinct, evident, intelligibility, limpid, lucidity, manifest, obvious, ostensibly, palpable, patently, pellucid, perceptible, perspicacity, ubiquitous ►abash, addle, anarchy, baffle, bamboozle, bedlam, bewilderment, confounded, derangement, din, discombobulated, disconcerted, moil, muddle, perplexed, pother, welter

Reality or Illusion
现实还是幻想

我们从电视广告中接收到的信息是真实的吗？还是说它们只是庞大的广告产业编织出的*幻境*（*fantasies*）？信息无时无刻不在狂轰滥炸，因此，我们必须根据信息的*真实性*（*validity*）或者*不准确性*（*inaccuracy*）对信息加以仔细地筛查和分类。我们的语言向我们提供了很多单词，帮助我们分清楚 *whimsy* 和 *bona fide truisms* 的区别。

actuality	genuine	tenable
applicable	invulnerable	truism
authenticity	legitimacy	unassailable
bona fide	materiality	valid
categorical	pragmatic	veracity
defensible	real McCoy	veritable
factual	tangible	

aberration	fallacy	inaccurate
artifice	fantasy	mirage
chimera	fleeting	phantasm
deceptive	hallucination	semblance
ephemeral	illusion	short-lived
erroneous	imaginative	transient
evanescent	imprecise	whimsy

▶ **actuality**
/ˌæktʃʊˈæləti/
n.

the state of being actual or real; truly existing 现实

On Halloween the children were so taken by the costumes that they had a difficult time distinguishing between *actuality* and pretend. 万圣节时，孩子们被各种服饰深深地迷惑住了，以至于很难分清楚是现实的世界还是装扮出来的世界。

adjective: **actual**

▶ **applicable**
/ˈæplɪkəbl̩/
a.

readily usable; practical 适用的

Lorena was not sure that her ideas were *applicable* to the problem, but she offered them, nevertheless. 洛雷纳不确定她的想法是否适用于这个问题，但她还是提了出来。

noun: **applicability**

▶ **authenticity**
/ˌɔθənˈtɪsəti/
n.

the quality or condition of being authentic, trustworthy, or genuine 真实性，确实性，可靠性

Before paying the high price for the Picasso painting, the art dealer had to check the *authenticity* of the work. 在出高价购买毕加索的画作之前，画商必须检验作品的真实性。

adjective: **authentic**
adverb: **authentically**

▶ **bona fide**
/ˈbonə ˈfaɪdɪ/
a.

• authentic and genuine 真正的，真实的

Among all the knockoffs in the shoe store, I found an inexpensive pair of *bona fide* Adidas. 在鞋店的无数冒牌货中，我找到了一双廉价的阿迪达斯正品鞋。

• made and carried out in good faith 充满诚意的

The offer on the farmhouse was a ***bona fide*** agreement; the seller and buyer shook hands to secure the deal. 出售农舍的协议充满诚意，买卖双方成交了这笔生意。

▶ **categorical**
/ˌkætə'gɔrɪkl̩/
a.

- without exception; absolute and explicit 绝对的

Nobody in the room doubted that Samuel was the ***categorical*** winner of the Lincoln-Douglas debate. 房间里没有人怀疑塞缪尔是林肯－道格拉斯辩论赛当之无愧的冠军。

- of or relating to categories or arrangement or order 分类的，与类别、安排、秩序有关的

Sammy was so left-brained, logical, and sequential that no one was surprised when she put all her information in precise, ***categorical*** order. 萨米左脑如此发达，讲究逻辑和次序，以至于当她把自己所有的信息都准确地归类时，没有人感到惊讶。

▶ **defensible**
/dɪ'fɛnsəbl̩/
a.

justifiable for accuracy 正当有理的，可辩解的

Maria had a ***defensible*** position: There was no doubt that she would win the debate. 玛丽亚的观点是站得住脚的：毫无疑问她将赢得这场辩论。

noun: **defensibility, defensibleness**
adverb: **defensibly**

▶ **factual**
/'fæktʃʊəl/
a.

of the nature of fact; real （基于）事实的；真实的

Even though the book was a work of fiction, it was full of ***factual*** information about that historical era. 尽管这是一本小说，但却充满了那个历史时期的史实。

noun: **factuality**
adverb: **factually**

► **genuine**
/'dʒɛnjuɪn/
a.

not counterfeit, but authentic; honest and real; free from hypocrisy or dishonesty; sincere 真正的，非伪造的；诚实可靠的；真诚的

My uncle gave me a *genuine* two-dollar bill for my birthday. 我叔叔送给我一张2美元的真币作为生日礼物。

noun: **genuineness**
adverb: **genuinely**

► **invulnerable**
/ɪn'vʌlnərəbl̩/
a.

impossible to damage or enter 无法伤害的；攻不破的；无懈可击的

The front door seemed *invulnerable*; it was made of steel, and it sported seven strong locks as well. 前门似乎是攻不破的，它是铁制的，而且还上了七把十分坚固的锁。

adverb: **invulnerably**
noun: **invulnerability**

► **legitimacy**
/lɪ'dʒɪtɪməsɪ/
n.

the quality of being legitimate — authentic, genuine, and according to the law 合法性，正当性

The painting was suspect, so the *legitimacy* of its authenticity was questionable. 这幅画十分可疑，因此它的真实性也很值得怀疑。

adverb: **legitimately**
adjective: **legitimate**

► **materiality**
/mə,tɪrɪ'ælətɪ/
n.

• the state of being material 物质（性）

Esther was so intent upon possessing things that her friends started questioning her focus on *materiality*. 埃丝特如此专注于拥有一切，以至于她的朋友们开始质疑她对物质的偏爱。

- being of real or substantive quality 实体性，有形性

In *Macbeth*, Banquo's ghost appears to Macbeth with such *materiality* that he is overwhelmed by guilt over Banquo's murder. 在《麦克白》中，班柯的鬼魂在麦克白看来是那么真实，以至于麦克白深深地陷入到因谋害班柯而产生的负罪感之中。

adjective: **material**
adverb: **materially**

▶ **pragmatic**
/præɡˈmætɪk/
a.

dealing with facts, reality, and actual occurrences 讲究实际的，务实的，重实效的

Aaron's insubstantial reasons were not *pragmatic*, so consequently no one believed him. 阿伦的理由很脆弱，一点都不切合实际，所以没有人相信他。

adverb: **pragmatically**
noun: **pragmatism**

▶ **real McCoy**
/ˈriəl məˈkɔɪ/
n.

an authentic thing or quality; something that is not an imitation or a substitute 真货；非仿品或替代品

The classic 1964 Ford Mustang was the *real McCoy*; not only had it not had any body work done on it, but it had never been repainted. 1964年产的经典"福特野马"的确货真价实；它不仅没有任何改装的痕迹，而且从来没有被重新喷过漆。

▶ **tangible**
/ˈtændʒəbl̩/
a.

possible to touch; possible to be treated as fact; real or concrete 可触摸到的；确凿的；真实的

Carlos's fantasy became *tangible* when Angie, the girl of his dreams, agreed to go out with him. 当卡洛斯的梦中情人安吉同意和他出去约会时，卡洛斯的幻想终于变成了现实。

noun: **tangibility**

adverb: **tangibly**

▶ **tenable**
/'tɛnəbl/

a.

capable of being maintained; able to be maintained because of genuineness 可保持一段时间的；有道理的，站得住脚的

The team's successful season was barely *tenable* because of the girls' growing apathy toward attending practice. 由于女孩们越来越不热衷于参加训练，这支队伍这一赛季的成功不太可能延续下去了。

adverb: **tenably**

▶ **truism**
/'truɪzəm/
n.

self-evident truth, actuality, and reality 自明之理，不言而喻的事实

The rumor about a possible scandal became a *truism* once the facts were released to the public. 一旦真相公之于众，流言蜚语也就不攻自破了。

▶ **unassailable**
/ˌʌnə'seləbl/
a.

undeniable, actual, and authentic 不容置疑的，真正的，可信的

The *unassailable* truth came out when Marla's little brother realized that their parents were really the Tooth Fairy. 当马拉的弟弟意识到牙仙真的是他们的父母的时候，事实的真相得以披露。

noun: **unassailability**

adverb: **unassailably**

▶ **valid**
/'vælɪd/
a.

real, authentic, correct; sound and well-grounded 有效的；有根据的；正确的

Benny Lee was able to draw a *valid* conclusion only after he had discovered all the facts. 本尼·李发现了所有的事实

之后，他才得出有根据的结论。

noun: **validity**
adverb: **validly**

▶ **veracity**
/vəˈræsətɪ/
n.

adherence to truth, reality, accuracy, and precision 真实

The teacher confirmed the *veracity* of the student's late pass by checking with the teacher who supposedly wrote the pass. 老师在与据称写了假条的那位老师核实之后，确认了学生迟到的假条是真的。

▶ **veritable**
/ˈverətəbl̩/
a.

being truly so-called; real or genuine 名副其实的；真正的

A *veritable* stranger was kind enough to give Suzanne enough money to use the phone so she could call home. 一个完全陌生的人好心地给了苏珊娜足够的钱，让她可以打电话回家。

adverb: **veritably**

· ·

▶ **aberration**
/ˌæbəˈreʃən/
n.

a defect or departure from the normal; deviation or imperfection 失常；背离

My mother was not sure whether her occasionally seeing her dead great grandmother was real or an *aberration*. 我妈妈不确定她偶尔看见她死去的曾祖母到底是真实的还是精神失常。

adjective: **aberrant**

▶ **artifice**
/ˈɑrtəfɪs/
n.

pretense, deception, or ruse 伪装，欺骗，诡计

The young woman was about 90 percent *artifice* and only 10 percent authentic. 这个年轻女人的行为90%具有欺骗性，

只有10%的可信。

adjective: **artificial**
adverb: **artificially**

▶ **chimera**
/kaɪˈmɪrə/
n.

• a fanciful mental illusion or fabrication 幻象；伪造物

The new history teacher seemed to be a *chimera*—one-half despot and one-half concerned mentor. 新来的历史老师似乎给人一种幻象——一半是专制的暴君，一半是关心学生的导师。

• an organism, organ, or part consisting of two or more tissues of different genetic composition 客迈拉（一种怪物）

The *chimera* of Greek mythology was a fire-breathing she monster who had a lion's head, a goat's body, and a snake's tail. 这个希腊神话中的妖怪是一个有狮头、羊身和蛇尾的吐火女怪。

▶ **deceptive**
/dɪˈsɛptɪv/
a.

tending to deceive, betray, or fool; unauthentic and untrue 欺骗的；不真实的

The burglar was *deceptive* because he left the front door unlocked, even though he entered and left the house from the rear. 这个窃贼非常具有欺骗性，尽管他是从后门进出房子，却把前门留在那儿没锁。

adverb: **deceptively**
noun: **deception**

▶ **ephemeral**
/əˈfɛmərəl/
a.

not real or authentic for any length of time; fleeting 短暂的，瞬息的

The thrill of tearing down a hill on a sled is *ephemeral* because soon you have to get off the sled and climb to the top of the hill again. 乘雪橇从山上滑下的兴奋感转瞬即逝，因为不久你就得从雪橇上下来并再一次爬到山顶。

▶ **erroneous**
/əˈronɪəs/

a.

mistaken and untrue 错误的，不真实的

Erroneous information led to the police force to pursue the wrong suspect. 错误的信息导致警察机关追错了嫌疑犯。

noun: **erroneousness**
adverb: **erroneously**

▶ **evanescent**
/ˌɛvəˈnɛsṇt/

a.

vanishing or likely to vanish; without much substance 迅速消失的，瞬息的，短暂的

One's dreams are often *evanescent*, because, soon after waking, most people forget the details. 梦境通常是迅速被遗忘的，因为梦醒后不久大多数人都不记得梦里的细节。

noun: **evanescence**
verb: **evanesce**

▶ **fallacy**
/ˈfæləsɪ/

n.

• a false notion 谬论

It is a *fallacy* to think black cats bring bad luck. 认为黑猫会带来霉运是无稽之谈。

• a rhetorical flaw in an argument 错误的推理

There was such a glaring *fallacy* in the lawyer's argument that it was no surprise that he lost the case. 这个律师的辩护中有一个非常明显的错误推理，无怪乎他输了官司。

• an untruth 谎言，假话

Some pessimists believe that true love is a *fallacy*; it just doesn't exist. 一些悲观主义者认为真爱是谎言，它根本不存在。

adjective: **fallacious**

▶ **fantasy**
/ˈfæntəsɪ/
n.

a creation of the imagination; an imagined event; a dream 幻想，想象

Tolkien is the author who introduced the reading public to a genre of fiction known as *fantasy* novels. 托尔金是将幻想小说流派带给大众读者的作家。

adjective: **fantastic, fantastical**
verb: **fantasize**

▶ **fleeting**
/ˈflitɪŋ/
a.

passing quickly; ephemeral 飞逝的；短暂的

We caught a *fleeting* glimpse at the squirrel as it scampered away from the bird feeder. 在这只松鼠从给食器旁蹦走的瞬间，我们瞥见了它。

adverb: **fleetingly**

▶ **hallucination**
/həˌlusn̩ˈeʃən/
n.

• a false or mistaken idea; a delusion 错觉，幻想

After my grandfather's death, my grandmother experienced some strong *hallucinations* in which her late husband talked to her. 我祖父死后，祖母总有一些很强烈的错觉，在错觉里已故的丈夫在对她讲话。

• a multisensory experience with no external stimulus, often drug-induced 幻觉（通常为药物所致）

While coming out of the anesthetic after my surgery, I kept having very strange *hallucinations*. 在手术后麻醉剂消散的过程中，我持续体验着很奇怪的幻觉。

adjective: **hallucinatory**
verb: **hallucinate**

▶**illusion**
/ɪˈluʒən/
a.

an erroneous perception of reality; a fantastical plan 错觉；幻想

Helen had a strong *illusion* about the possibility of someone following her. 海伦有种很强的错觉，认为可能有人在跟踪她。

adjective: **illusionary**

▶**imaginative**
/ɪˈmædʒənetɪv/
a.

having a lively, creative mind; creating fantastic dreams 富于想象力的；运用想象力的

imaginary
/ɪˈmædʒənɛrɪ/
a.

not real, from the imagination 假想的，虚构的

It is not unusual for a child, especially an only child, to be very *imaginative* and to create an *imaginary* friend. 小孩子，尤其是独生子女，通常是极富想象力的，他们常常会虚构一个想象中的朋友。

adverb: **imaginatively**
verb: **imagine**

▶**imprecise**
/ˌɪmprɪˈsaɪs/
a.

not precise; not exact or sure 不精确的，不确切的

Since Mallory's answer was rather *imprecise*, Mathew's response sounded intelligent and specific by comparison. 与马洛里很不准确的回答相比，马修的回答很机智、很具体。

noun: **imprecision**
adverb: **imprecisely**

▶**inaccurate**
/ɪnˈækjərɪt/

mistaken or incorrect; not accurate 不正确的；不精确的

a. Abraham stood by his beliefs and principles whether they were *inaccurate* or exact. 亚伯拉罕坚持自己的信仰和原则，无论准确与否。

noun: **inaccuracy**
adverb: **inaccurately**

▶ **mirage**
/mə'rɑʒ/
n.

• something that is illusory or insubstantial 幻想，妄想

Thomas always visualized the *mirage* of a six-figure income. 托马斯经常幻想自己的工资是六位数。

• an optical phenomenon that creates the illusion of water 海市蜃楼

A typical *mirage* is a green and lush oasis in the middle of a desert. 典型的海市蜃楼是在沙漠中心有一座葱翠的绿洲。

▶ **phantasm**
/'fæntæzəm/
n.

something apparently seen but without any true physical presence; an illusion of the brain; a ghost or spirit 幻影，幻觉，幻象；鬼魂

Despite the reaction from others, Paula wasn't sure if she was experiencing a real explanation for what had happened, or just a *phantasm* of her imagination. 尽管别人也有所反应，可葆拉仍然不确定她正经历的是真实发生的事情，抑或仅仅是自己的幻觉。

adjective: **phantasmal**

▶ **semblance**
/'sɛmbləns/
n.

outward appearance; a representation or a copy of something else 外表，外观；类似，相似

Although the students were very excited, the principal was able to get them into some *semblance* of order. 尽管学生们很激动，但校长还是让大家都维持住了表面的秩序。

adjective: **semblable**

▶ **short-lived**
/'ʃɔrt'lɪvd/
a.

living or lasting only a short while; fleeting 持续不久的，短暂的

The team's 2-point lead was short-lived, for soon the other team got two baskets in a row. 这支队伍两分的领先优势很短暂，不久另一支队便连续两个投篮命中。

▶ **transient**
/'trænʃənt/
a.,n.

adjective: passing in time; remaining or existing only briefly 短暂的，一时的

When I was growing up, my family led a *transient* life. 我小时候跟家人过着居无定所的生活。

noun: one who passes through without permanent bonds 短期居留者

When I was growing up I was a *transient*, because my father was in the U.S. Air Force; we moved to a new place every two or three years. 由于父亲在美国空军服役，小时候的我是个短暂居住者，每两三年都会搬一个新地方。

adverb: **transiently**

▶ **whimsy**
/'hwɪmzɪ/
n.

a whim or an odd or fanciful idea; sometimes a quaint or unorthodox idea 荒诞的想法，怪念头

Acting upon mere *whimsy*, Francis went to talk to the assistant principal, and his plans were, surprisingly, approved. 一个不经意的怪念头使弗朗西斯找到副校长谈话，出乎意料的是他的方案获准了。

adjective: **whimsical**
adverb: **whimsically**

Sentence Completion 完成句子

Circle the word or word pair that best completes the meaning of the sentence. 圈出最符合句子含义的词或一对词。

1. The accused man's lawyer had to create a _____ case that would be _____ to the attack of the prosecuting attorney.
   A. defensible/invulnerable
   B. categorical/pragmatic
   C. factual/ephemeral
   D. valid/erroneous
   E. genuine/tenable

2. My uncle led a very _____ life; he would come and go, based solely on whatever _____ controlled him at that time.
   A. genuine/materiality
   B. categorical/chimera
   C. transient/whimsy
   D. unassailable/aberration
   E. defensible/truism

3. The oasis in the desert was just a _____, only a _____, or an illusion of green on the endless sand and under the unforgiving sun.
   A. whimsy/short-lived
   B. mirage/phantasm
   C. legitimacy/real McCoy
   D. aberration/fallacy
   E. chimera/actuality

4. Flora made a(n) _____ assumption about her teacher; after a couple months she realized he was _____ interested in his students above everything else.

A. applicable/pragmatically

B. actual/categorically

C. erroneous/genuinely

D. invulnerable/whimsically

E. whimsical/transiently

5. The coach's favor with the public was _____; once the team started losing games, his fans' belief in him was only _____ — here today and gone tomorrow.

A. semblance/authentic

B. transient/fleeting

C. hallucinatory/imprecise

D. inaccurate/legitimate

E. invulnerable/phantasmal

Quick Matching 快速配对

Write the letter of the definition shown in the right column next to the word that matches it in the left column. 在右栏中找出与左栏单词相符的定义，将对应的字母写在单词旁。

_____1. categorical	A. capable of being maintained
_____2. materiality	B. justifiable accuracy
_____3. veracity	C. self-evident, actually
_____4. tenable	D. a reality of substance
_____5. defensible	E. absolute, explicit, and without exception

Complete the Story 完成故事

Using these words selected from this unit, fill in the blanks to complete the story. 用本单元的词汇填空，完成故事。

categorical	unassailable
genuine	pragmatic
fleeting	fallacious
legitimate	deceptive
artifice	tangible
tenable	chimera
evanescent	mirage
legitimacy	legitimate
actuality	bona fide
whimsy	ephemeral
imaginative	valid
veracity	

The art and _____ of the advertisement business is a _____ study of _____ and _____ versus the _____ and the _____. Advertising itself is a _____, a union of two opposites. Nowhere else in our lives are so many promises offered to us than through the world of ads. We are not supposed to consider how _____ and without substance these promises really are. Instead, consumers are supposed to accept what they are told as _____ information, _____ truths, and _____ hopes based upon _____ facts.

In reality, advertising is the business of building for us a supposedly _____ world in which we are promised _____ _____ improvements to our lives, to our families, and to all that we consider important. If we experience momentary, _____ doubts about a product's assurances, we quickly shift our minds and pretend that it was simply an _____ perception or even a _____ that never existed as a real, _____ thought. Advertisers do not want their viewing public to be _____. They convince us of the _____ of their claims; they offer us _____, short-lived promises, convincing us with _____ arguments and gentle persuasion. Consumers, unfortunately, are often immune to such ploys, and they rush right out to their latest, have-to-have _____.

ANSWERS 答案

Sentence Completion 完成句子：1-A, 2-C, 3-B, 4-C, 5-B

Quick Matching 快速配对：1-E, 2-D, 3-B, 4-A, 5-C

Complete the Story 完成故事：artifice, categorical, actuality, veracity, imaginative, deceptive, chimera, evanescent, valid, unassailable, tenable, tangible, genuine, bona fide, fleeting, erroneous, mirage, legitimate, pragmatic, legitimacy, ephemeral, fallacious, whimsy

How Often?
有多经常?

你有没有填过这样的问卷，让你衡量做某件事情的频率？例如，一份关于看电视的习惯的问卷可能会问你是*经常*（*often*）、*有时候*（*occasionally*）、*偶尔*（*once in a while*）、*很少*（*rarely*）还是*从来不*（*never*）看体育赛事。我想你明白我指的是哪种问卷。下面是一系列问卷设计者很可能从未听说过的词。也许你可以把它们凑在一起，制作自己的频率问卷。毫无疑问，你可以比大多数专业问卷设计者做得更好。

contingent	interrupt	spasmodic
episodic	oscillate	sporadic
incidental	periodic	transitory
intermittent	recurrent	vacillate

....

chronic	indefatigable	persevering
coherent	insistent	persistent
habitual	inveterate	resistant
incessant	perpetual	unremitting

► **contingent** • liable to occur but not with certainty; possible 偶然发生
/kən'tɪndʒənt/ 的；可能的
a.

Today's weather forecast includes a ***contingent*** chance of showers by evening. 天气预报显示今天夜间偶或有阵雨。

• dependent on conditions or occurrences not yet established 临时的，视条件而定的

My cousin is a ***contingent*** worker; she works for a temporary employment agency. 我表姐是临时工，她在一个临时的雇佣机构上班。

noun: **contingency**

► **episodic** relating to or happening in episodes （小说、剧本等）由
/ˌɛpɪ'sɑdɪk/ 片段组成的
a.

The made-for-television movie was ***episodic***; that is, it was broadcast in sections rather than all in one night. 这段专门为在电视上播放而制作的电影是由片段组成的。也就是说，它并不是集中在一个晚上完整播放，而是分成几部分播出。

adverb: **episodically**

► **incidental** apt to occur in a minor or unpredictable manner 不重要的；偶
/ˌɪnsə'dɛntl̩/ 发的
a.

It was an ***incidental*** bother; only rarely did the turn signal stick while I was driving. 汽车转向灯出故障只会偶尔发生，我开车时很少遇到。

adverb: **incidentally**

► **intermittent** stopping and starting at intervals 断断续续的

/ˌɪntəˈmɪtn̩t/
a.

The news about the disaster was *intermittent*; the network fed the public information only a little at a time. 关于灾难事故的报导是断断续续的，网络每次只给公众提供一点信息。

noun: **intermittence**
adverb: **intermittently**

▶ **interrupt**
/ˌɪntəˈrʌpt/
v.

to break the rhythm or continuity; to stop the momentum or continuum 中断；暂时中止

Because of the lightning, the officials had to *interrupt* the game. 由于闪电的缘故，官员不得不中断这场比赛。

adjective: **interrupted**
noun: **interruption**

▶ **oscillate**
/ˈɑsl̩ˌet/
v.

to move back and forth; to waver or doubt a decision 有规律地来回摆动；动摇不定，怀疑

It was a hot night, and the air conditioner in the house broke down. Even the fan wouldn't *oscillate*. It just sat there, not turning, just pushing the hot air out in front of it. 那天晚上很热，房间的空调也坏了。就连风扇都不转了，只是立在那儿，挡住跟前的热空气。

noun: **oscillation**
adjective: **oscillating**

▶ **periodic**
/ˌpɪrɪˈɑdɪk/
a.

characterized by a repeating cycle or repetition of intervals; appearing or occurring from time to time 定期的

Her visits to her grandparents are *periodic*. Although there is no formal agreement with them, she visits nearly every other weekend. 她会定期去拜访祖父母。尽管没有正式

约定，但每隔一周她就会在周末去一次。

adverb: **periodically**

▶ **recurrent**
/rɪˈkɝənt/
a.

occurring repeatedly 一再发生的

Martha kept having a ***recurrent*** dream; night after night she had the same nightmare. 玛莎反复做着同一个梦，每晚都被这个噩梦困扰。

adverb: **recurrently**
noun: **recurrence**

▶ **spasmodic**
/spæzˈmɑdɪk/
a.

• having the characteristic of a spasm or convulsion 阵发性的，痉挛（性）的

The medication caused the patient to experience ***spasmodic*** episodes. 药物使患者出现阵发性痉挛。

• happening intermittently; from time to time 断断续续的，一阵阵的

The ***spasmodic*** sound of fireworks frightened the dog. 一阵阵的烟花爆竹声吓着了这只狗。

adverb: **spasmodically**
noun: **spasm**

▶ **sporadic**
/spəˈrædɪk/
a.

occurring at different intervals, with no set pattern 偶尔发生的，零星的，分散的

The rain has been ***sporadic*** this summer, so people have to water their yards and gardens more often than in past summers. 今年夏天雨水少，因而与往年夏天相比，人们得多给庭院和花园浇些水。

adverb: **sporadically**

▶ **transitory**
/ˈtrænsəˌtɔrɪ/
a.

short-lived; temporary; only passing, not permanent 短暂的，瞬息的

Josh was involved in yet another of his *transitory* love affairs; this was his fifth girlfriend in two months. 乔希又谈了场短暂的恋爱，这是他两个月中交的第五个女朋友。

▶ **vacillate**
/ˈvæslˌet/
v.

to move back and forth, especially being unable to make up one's mind 踌躇，举棋不定

Michele *vacillated* constantly. She was so bad about making decisions that it took her three hours just to go grocery shopping. 米歇尔总是举棋不定。让她做个决定简直太难了，哪怕去食品店买东西都要花去三个小时。

adjective: **vacillating**
noun: **vacillation**

⋯⋯⋯⋯⋯⋯⋯⋯⋯⋯⋯⋯⋯⋯⋯⋯⋯⋯⋯⋯⋯⋯⋯

▶ **chronic**
/ˈkrɑnɪk/
a.

of long duration or frequent recurrence; happening a great deal and/or often（疾病）慢性的，长期的；反复出现的

Bronchitis is usually characterized by a *chronic* cough that often causes the sufferer great discomfort and extreme exhaustion. 通常支气管炎症状为长期咳嗽，这种咳嗽经常会使患者非常不适和极度疲劳。

noun: **chronicity**
adverb: **chronically**

▶ **coherent**
/koˈhɪrənt/
a.

marked by an orderly, logical, consistent relationship; not broken up by distraction or intervening time or information; consistent 连贯的，有条理的，前后一致的

The information has been *coherent*. For once the media have reported the facts as they occur, with few confusing asides. 信息前后连贯、一致。因为事情在发生之初便有媒体报导，所以混淆视听的言论很少。

noun: **coherence**
adverb: **coherently**
verb: **cohere**

► **habitual**
/hə'bɪtʃʊəl/
a.

naturally out of habit or routine; regular and common 习惯（性）的，惯常的

Sonnen was a *habitual* nail-biter during stressful times, so it was not unusual for her fingertips to bleed by the time she finished a challenging exam. 索南一紧张就会习惯性地咬指甲，因此她在参加完挑战性强的考试后指尖流血也就不足为奇了。

adverb: **habitually**
noun: **habit**

► **incessant**
/ɪn'sɛsn̩t/
a.

continuing without interruption, sometimes to an excessive degree 持续不断的

The *incessant* rain was beginning to drive people stir-crazy; they were hoping for a break in the weather so they could get outside for a while. 雨下起来没完没了，人们开始崩溃，都期望着天气能短暂放晴，好出门溜达一下。

noun: **incessancy**
adverb: **incessantly**

► **indefatigable**
/ˌɪndɪ'fætɪgəbl̩/
a.

incapable of becoming tired or ceasing; not stopping or giving up 不倦的，不停歇的；不屈不挠的；不放弃的

The park ranger seemed to be *indefatigable*; long after

everyone else was exhausted, he kept up his steady pace. 这位公园管理员似乎不知疲倦，其余人早就筋疲力尽了，他却依然步履稳健。

adverb: **indefatigably**

▶ **insistent**
/ɪn'sɪstənt/
a.

firm in asserting a demand or an opinion; unyielding; repetitive 坚持的，执拗的；不屈服的；重复的

The crows' *insistent* cries in the early morning made sleeping nearly impossible for anyone in the area. 清晨乌鸦持续不断的叫声让这一区域的人们很难继续入睡。

noun: **insistence**
adverb: **insistently**
verb: **insist**

▶ **inveterate**
/ɪn'vetərɪt/
a.

long established; habitual 根深蒂固的；习惯的

I never trust anything she says — the woman is an inveterate liar. 我从不信她说的话——这个女人是个惯于说谎的人。

adverb: **inveterately**

▶ **perpetual**
/pɚ'petʃuəl/
a.

continuing or lasting for an indefinitely long or unlimited period of time 无休止的，连续不断的

The *perpetual* motion clock in the science building never needs winding or attention, because the earth's gravity is what keeps it going. 在地球引力的作用下，科技楼上的机械钟从不需要上发条或照管就可以无休止地走下去。

adverb: **perpetually**
verb: **perpetuate**

▶ **persevering**
/ˌpɜːsəˈvɪrɪŋ/
a.

to persist in or remain constant to a purpose, idea, or task; not giving up or giving in to obstacles 锲而不舍的，坚持不懈的

Henri's *persevering* nature enabled him to graduate with honors despite having no support or encouragement from friends or family. 尽管没有家人或朋友的支持和鼓励，但亨利凭着锲而不舍的精神以优异的成绩毕业了。

noun: **perseverance**
adverb: **perseveringly**
verb: **persevere**

▶ **persistent**
/pɚˈsɪstənt/
a.

not letting up; continuing even to the point of being bothersome 持续的；不断的；固执的

Nathan found that the *persistent* spam he kept getting on his computer was enough to cause him to change his Internet carrier. 内森受够了他电脑里持续不断接收到的垃圾邮件，决意换个网络载体。

noun: **persistence**
adverb: **persistently**
verb: **persist**

▶ **resistant**
/rɪˈzɪstənt/
a.

not giving up or giving in; fighting against the odds 不放弃的；不屈服的；抵抗的

The watch I received when I was 10 years old was so *resistant* to damage that I was still wearing it when I graduated from high school. 我10岁那年收到的那块手表特别抗损耐磨，直到高中毕业我还戴着它。

noun: **resistance**
verb: **resist**

► **unremitting** never slackening or getting any less or any easier; persistent
/ˌʌnrɪˈmɪtɪŋ/   坚持不懈的，持续的
a.

George's grudge was so *unremitting* that, long after he had
forgotten the reason for their quarrel, he would still not talk
to his cousin Arturo. 连争吵的原因都忘记了很久后，乔
治的怨恨依旧很深，还是不愿与堂弟阿图罗说话。

noun: **unremittingness**
adverb: **unremittingly**

Sentence Completion 完成句子

Circle the word or word pair that best completes the meaning of the sentence. 圈出最符合句子含义的词或一对词。

1. The company's plans to move forward were not solid because everything was _____ upon its client's acceptance of the offer.
   A. recurrent
   B. contingent
   C. incessant
   D. coherent
   E. insistent

2. The child followed the back-and-forth playground taunts with the _____ attention of a tennis referee.
   A. inveterate
   B. intermittent
   C. interrupted
   D. oscillating
   E. spasmodic

3. The television news _____ the program _____ with information about the increasing devastation caused by the hurricane.
   A. interrupted/periodically
   B. perpetuated/persistently
   C. resisted/recurrently
   D. vacillated/chronically
   E. insisted/intermittently

4. The toddler's _____ crying finally diminished to a _____ whimper.

A. indefatigable/inveterate

B. spasmodic/coherent

C. resistant/persevering

D. incessant/intermittent

E. chronic/perpetual

5. The guerrilla attacks were _____, _____ about once a month.

A. spasmodic/oscillating

B. chronic/cohering

C. incessant/interrupting

D. sporadic/vacillating

E. episodic/recurring

Quick Matching 快速配对

Write the letter of the definition shown in the right column next to the word that matches it in the left column. 在右栏中找出与左栏单词相符的定义，将对应的字母写在单词旁。

_____1. spasmodic   A. continuity being broken

_____2. persistent   B. fighting against all odds

_____3. perpetual   C. seeming to have no end in sight

_____4. resistant   D. happening from time to time

_____5. interrupted   E. continuing in a bothersome manner

Complete the Story 完成故事

Using these words selected from this unit, fill in the blanks to complete the story. 用本单元的词汇填空，完成故事。

resistant	indefatigable
episodic	vacillates
sporadic	insists
insistent	contingent
unremitting	consistently
persistently	oscillate

My best friends, Mack and Mike, are as opposite as two people can be. Whenever they are faced with decisions, Mack gets right on the situation, but Mike is wishy-washy and _____ undecided. Despite Mack's nagging, Mike is _____ to any resolution whatsoever. Whenever he is expected to make up his mind, he _____ between his choices and only rarely can he settle on an option. In contrast, Mack is always quick to decide and act. He _____ that he knows what he wants. He _____ bugs Mike to hurry up and make up his mind. In fact, he is such an _____ pest, so unrelenting in his urging, that he and Mike have often nearly come to blows over Mack's _____ clamor for his friend to just make up his mind.

Despite their differences, I am never torn in my affection toward either friend. Their contrasting behavior is so _____ that I can almost set my calendar by it. I've come to realize that Mike will _____ back and forth while trying to make up his mind. His responses always seem to be _____ upon one thing or another. On the other hand, Mack is a rock;

his decisiveness is _____; there is nothing haphazard or
_____ in any of his actions.

ANSWERS 答案
Sentence Completion 完成句子: 1-B, 2-D, 3-A, 4-D, 5-E
Quick Matching 快速配对: 1-D, 2-E, 3-C, 4-B, 5-A
Complete the Story 完成故事: consistently, resistant,
vacillates, insists, persistently, insistent, unremitting,
episodic, oscillate, contingent, indefatigable, sporadic

In Order of Importance
按照重要性排序

我们经常需要强调一件事情比另一件事情更重要，或者一件事情比另一件事情意义更重大。如果说我们刚看的电影还不错 (*okay*)，或者家庭作业*很重要* (*important*)，或者涨津贴*非常非常重要* (*really, really important*)，这并不能告诉我们其中的细微区别。下面一些词可以帮助你形容不重要的事情，也可以让你很好地描述非常重要的事情。

extraneous	insubstantial	subordinate
immaterial	irrelevant	subsidiary
impalpable	jot	whit
incidental	modicum	
inconsequential	nonessential	

....

abstruse	noteworthy	rarefied
considerable	poignant	significant
estimable	portend	substantial
intense	portentous	
momentous	profound	

▶ **extraneous**
/ɪk'strenɪəs/
a.

• having no vital importance 不重要的，无关的

Because we already had enough volunteers for the job, Charles's presence was *extraneous*. 因为我们已经为这项工作招足了志愿者，因此查尔斯的到场并不重要。

• coming from the outside; not innate 外部的，外来的

When developing a successful argument, you want to stick to the facts and avoid *extraneous* bits of information. 成功的辩论需要用事实说话，应避免选取无关的外部信息。

adverb: **extraneously**

▶ **immaterial**
/ˌɪmə'tɪrɪəl/
a.

• of no importance; beside the point 不重要的；不相干的

The piece of information that Sonya offered was *immaterial* to the solution. 索尼娅提供的消息对解决问题起不到作用。

• having no material substance 无形的，非物质的

Those who talk about angels have trouble explaining their *immaterial* form. 人们很难解释"天使"这种非物质的存在形式。

adverb: **immaterially**

▶ **impalpable**
/ɪm'pælpəbl̩/
a.

not able to be grasped, held, or understood 触摸不着的，感觉不到的；难懂的

For many who struggle with mathematics, the concept of negative numbers is as *impalpable* as trying to distinguish the individual grains that make up talcum powder. 对于学数学很吃力的人来说，负数的概念就如同辨别滑石粉的组成颗粒一样难以感知。

adverb: **impalpably**
noun: **impalpability**

▶ **incidental**   having little or no importance or impact 不重要的
/ˌɪnsə'dɛntl̩/
    a.   The earthquake was so mild that most people in San
    Francisco considered it of *incidental* importance. 这次地
    震的震感非常微弱，旧金山的人们并不觉得有什么大
    不了。

    adverb: **incidentally**
    noun: **incident**

▶ **inconsequential** • lacking importance 不重要的，无足轻重的
/ˌɪnkɑnsə'kwɛnʃəl/
    a.   Because the law was revoked, the argument became
    inconsequential and the protestors returned home. 这一争议
    在该法律被宣告无效后显得不重要了，于是抗议者们都
    回家了。

    • not following from premises or evidence; illogical 不合逻
    辑的

    Because of several logical fallacies in the argument, the
    debater's conclusion became *inconsequential*. 由于论据中
    存在多项逻辑错误，该辩论者的结论显得很没道理。

    adverb: **inconsequentially**

▶ **insubstantial** • negligible in size, importance, or strength 微不足道的
/ˌɪnsəb'stænʃəl/• • delicate; flimsy; without substance 柔弱的，脆弱的；无
    a.   实体的

    Because Jason had not yet experienced his adolescent
    growth spurt, he was too *insubstantial* to play football for
    his junior high school. 贾森还没经历青春期的快速发育，
    因此瘦弱的他还不能代表自己的中学去踢球。

noun: **insubstantiality**

▶ **irrelevant** unrelated to the matter being considered 不相干的，不相
/ɪˈrɛləvənt/ 关的
a.

Because José had little experience in the art of social conversation, he frequently made *irrelevant*, sometimes absurd, statements that would often bring the conversation to a standstill. 乔斯的社交经验太少，经常谈一些毫不相关、有时甚至荒唐的话题，使得交流无法继续进行。

adverb: **irrelevantly**
noun: **irrelevance**

▶ **jot** noun: a very small bit; an iota 一点儿；很少量
/dʒɑt/

n., v. The teacher did not care a *jot* about the student's hundredth excuse for being late. 老师并不理睬这个学生因迟到而编造了的无数理由。

verb: to make a quick note; to write down a few things 匆匆记下；做少量记录

Whenever Stephen King has a brainstorm for another story, he *jots* down his thoughts so that he won't forget them. 斯蒂芬·金一构思出一个新故事就会用笔记下来，以防遗忘。

▶ **modicum** a small, very modest, or token amount 少量，一点点
/ˈmɑdɪkəm/

n. The least we should do is give the speaker a *modicum* of attention, even though she is boring us to tears. 尽管她讲得无聊透顶，我们至少也应稍微听一听。

▶ **nonessential** not essential; of little or trivial importance 不重要的
/nɑnəˈsɛnʃəl/

a.   Often, when you search something on the Internet, you discover a lot of *nonessential* information before you find what's really important to your quest. 上网搜资料的通常情况是：在发现真正重要的信息前会遇到一堆没用的信息。

▶ **subordinate**   adjective: inferior in position to another 下级的
/sə'bɔrdn̩ɪt/

a., n.   As a new private in the U.S. Army, Patrick was in a *subordinate* position to everyone else. 作为美军的一名新兵，帕特里克的军衔低于其他人。

noun: the position of inferiority 下级，下属

The rank of private is the rank of a *subordinate* because it is the lowest rank in the army. 二等兵这一军衔位于次等地位，因为它是军队的最低军衔。

adverb: **subordinately**
noun: **subordination**

▶ **subsidiary**   adjective: serving or augmenting another; of secondary
/səb'sɪdɪˌɛrɪ/   importance 附带的，从属的；次要的
a., n

That additional information is *subsidiary* to the specific facts of the case. 附加信息对这个案件的具体事实起辅助作用。

noun: that which is in the service or augmentation of something larger 子公司，附属机构

The kiosk on the ground level of the mall is a *subsidiary* to the department store on the second level. 购物中心一楼的货摊附属于二楼的百货商店。

▶ **whit**   the least bit; just an iota 少量，一点
/hwɪt/

n.

The child's blatant misbehavior made it clear that he did not give a *whit* about the consequences of what he was doing. 这个小孩不懂礼貌的肆意喧闹明显说明他对自己做的事从不考虑后果。

••

▶ **abstruse**
/əb'strus/
a.

not clear; ambiguous or uncertain; sometimes highbrow and totally beyond the norm 模糊不清的；深奥的，难懂的

The witness gave such an unimaginable and *abstruse* description of what he saw that the jury found him totally unconvincing. 目击证人对他所看到的事情的描述模糊不清并且超出常理，因此陪审团认为他的话不可信。

adverb: **abstrusely**

▶ **considerable**
/kən'sɪdərəbl̩/
a.

in a large or impressive amount or significance 相当多的；很重要的

The evidence of the crime was so *considerable* that most spectators expected the jury to quickly bring back a guilty verdict. 犯罪证据已经相当多了，所以大部分观看庭审的人都希望陪审团尽快做出有罪判定。

adverb: **considerably**

▶ **estimable**
/'ɛstəməbl̩/
a.

• capable of being estimated 可估计的

The *estimable* value of the widow's fortune was well over $1 million. 这位寡妇的财产估计超过100万美元。

• of considerable importance, influence, or esteem 受人瞩目的

The homecoming queen was of such *estimable* importance to the homecoming pageant that everyone wanted to be noticed by her. 在归国的盛装游行上，女王是如此受人瞩

目，以至于每个人都希望自己被她看到。

noun: **estimation**
adverb: **estimably**

▶ **intense**
/ɪnˈtɛns/
a.

• of extreme degree, characteristics, strength, or effort 强烈的，剧烈的，极度的

The fire was too *intense* for the firefighters to remain in the building. 大火烧得太猛烈，消防队员无法继续待在楼里。

• tending to feel deeply or profoundly 热切的，感情强烈的

Her mourning for her lost child became so *intense* that she needed to be sedated. 孩子的死使她过于悲痛，必须使用镇静剂才能安静下来。

noun: **intensity**
adverb: **intensely**

▶ **momentous**
/moˈmɛntəs/
a.

significant and meaningful; sometimes even historically important 重要的；重大的

The quarterback made a *momentous* decision when he opted to pass the ball, which led to Notre Dame winning the championship. 四分卫在传球的时候做了一个重要选择，最终使圣母队夺冠。

adverb: **momentously**
noun: **moment**

▶ **noteworthy**
/ˈnotˌwɝˈðɪ/
a.

something worth noting or paying attention to; significant; meaningful 值得注意的；重要的；有意义的

It was a *noteworthy* occasion when the governor of the state spoke at her daughter's high school graduation. 州长在她女儿高中毕业典礼上发表讲话，这是一个值得关注的重大时刻。

noun: **noteworthiness**

▶ **poignant**
/ˈpɔɪnjənt/
a.

important; moving; often emotionally significant 重要的；深深打动人的

After the 9/11 tragedy, the ceremony to honor the fallen victims, televised from the National Cathedral in Washington, D.C., was clearly a *poignant* experience for all who were involved. "9·11"事件后，华盛顿国家大教堂为遇难者举行的悼念仪式通过电视播送出来，这对于所有相关人士而言无疑是场深刻的经历。

adverb: **poignantly**
noun: **poignance**

▶ **portend**
/pɔrˈtɛnd/
v.

to foresee and/or foretell; to have an inclination about the future 预言；预知未来

The witches in *Macbeth* **portended** that Macbeth would become king; little did he know how dearly he would pay for their prediction. 《麦克白》中的女巫预言麦克白将成为国王；麦克白丝毫不知他将为女巫们的预言付出多大代价。

▶ **portentous**
/pɔrˈtɛntəs/
n.

significant, usually in a threatening or ominous way; filled with heavy misgiving 凶兆的，征兆不祥的

The sky looked **portentous** with its unusual brownish green aura, and soon we heard the sound of the tornado sirens. 罕见的褐绿色的天空暗藏凶兆，不久我们便听到了龙卷风警报声。

adverb: **portentously**

noun: **portent**

▶ **profound**
/prə'faʊnd/
a.

weighty; insightful; intense; full of meaning or significance 深刻的，意义深远的

Her mother's death when she was aged seven had a very *profound* effect on her. 7岁时妈妈去世对她影响巨大。

adverb: **profoundly**

noun: **profoundly**

▶ **rarefied**
/'rɛrəfaɪd/
a.

belonging to a select or even lofty group; elevated in character; esoteric 只限于少数的

My uncle was pledged to a fraternity so *rarefied* that all members had to have at least a 170 IQ in order to belong. 我叔叔宣誓加入了一个兄弟会。这个兄弟会只面向很小的群体，只有智商在170以上的人才能加入。

noun: **rarefaction**

▶ **significant**
/sɪg'nɪfəkənt/
a.

of considerable importance or weighty concern 重要的，引人关注的

We could tell that our summons to the principal's office was *significant* because of Mr. Lewis's formality when we entered the room. 当我们进入校长办公室受到刘易斯先生的正式接待时，便意识到了这次召见的重要性。

adverb: **significantly**

noun: **significance**

▶ **substantial**
/səb'stænʃəl/
a.

ample; considerable; sizable; of substance; sometimes even weighty or large in size 大量的，可观的

The crowds that gathered for the protest were *substantial*, so the local police had to call on support from a neighboring jurisdiction to help with crowd control. 抗议人群数量庞大，当地警方不得不求助于邻近辖区，以对现场进行控制。

adverb: **substantially**
noun: **substantiation**

Sentence Completion 完成句子

Circle the word or word pair that best completes the meaning of the sentence. 圈出最符合句子含义的词或一对词。

1. During the funeral, emotions became _____; there wasn't a dry eye in the church.
   A. subordinate
   B. rarefied
   C. intense
   D. considerable
   E. portentous

2. The prosecutor's case fell apart after the police questioned all the witnesses and found their testimony to be not only contradictory but also _____.
   A. rarefied
   B. significant
   C. nonessential
   D. insubstantial
   E. impalpable

3. During the Fourth of July celebration, there was such _____ noise that my mother was unable to find a _____ of quiet amidst the pandemonium.
   A. abstruse/modicum
   B. substantial/whit
   C. poignant/subordinate
   D. noteworthy/jot
   E. incidental/irrelevance

4. Since everyone had already brought a _____ amount food to the picnic, Martha's single bag of chips was _____.
   A. considerable/immaterial
   B. portentous/subordinate
   C. momentous/impalpable
   D. profound/subsidiary
   E. rarefied/insubstantial

5. The research scientist's _____ discovery of a possible cure for a unique strain of AIDS brought _____ funding to the research lab.
   A. considerable/subsidiary
   B. noteworthy/substantial
   C. incidental/profound
   D. rarefied/immaterial
   E. estimable/extraneous

Quick Matching 快速配对

Write the letter of the definition shown in the right column next to the word that matches it in the left column. 在右栏中找出与左栏单词相符的定义，将对应的字母写在单词旁。

_____1. extraneous	A.	something of little or inconsequential importance
_____2. jot	B.	of no importance or significance
_____3. rarefied	C.	of considerable esteem or importance
_____4. subsidiary	D.	secondary or subordinate to another
_____5. estimable	E.	unusually awesome or out of the ordinary

Complete the Story 完成故事

Using these words selected from this unit, fill in the blanks to complete the story. 用本单元的词汇填空，完成故事。

rarefied	intense
substantial	poignant
subsidiary	profound
momentous	noteworthy
significant	jot
profound	inconsequential
extraneous	portentous
abstruse	incidental
considerable	

Mark, Jamie, and Rachelle were teamed together to do an important, _____ research project on the _____ ruin of Stonehenge. They had no idea how _____ the work would be. At first, Jamie thought that the assignment was not worth much and was _____, but then the teacher informed them that this project would be worth 25 percent of their semester grade. Suddenly, what had seemed like just one more _____ busywork activity was now a _____ part of their grade.

It did not take the three of them long to realize that no one knew a _____ about the monument or its _____ significance to early British history. As each of the team members discovered _____ pieces of information, what seemed insignificant suddenly became _____.

After they collected a _____ amount of information,

they organized it into an estimable outline of facts, but some were too confusing and _____ to use, and others became _____ to the primary focus of the project. After weeks of collaboration, the _____ deadline arrived, and they turned in their project. After they breathed a sigh of relief, they looked at one another and felt good about what they had accomplished. It was a very _____ moment for them all. Rather than having _____ misgivings about their efforts, they all felt a _____ relief at a job well done.

ANSWERS 答案

Sentence Completion 完成句子： 1-C, 2-D, 3-B, 4-A, 5-B

Quick Matching 快速配对： 1-B, 2-A, 3-E, 4-D, 5-C

Complete the Story 完成故事： significant, rarefied, intense, inconsequential, extraneous, substantial, jot, profound, incidental, noteworthy, considerable, abstruse, subsidiary, momentous, poignant, portentous, profound

Crystal Clear and Sure or Shadowy, Uncertain, and Disturbed
非常清楚的和确定的，难以捉摸的、不确定的和不安的

就算是有条不紊的人也会因意料之外的事情而烦躁不安。打个比方，被打乱了的旅行计划往往会把最有条理最*明确*（*lucid*）的安排变成一*团乱麻*（*muddled bedlam*）。甚至那些展现了计划者的才华（*intelligibility*）和聪慧（*perspicacity*)的清晰的（*patently obvious*)计划也会出差错。当原本*明确的*（*distinct*）计划出于某种原因不得不在表面上（*ostensibly*）有所调整时，这一点就格外*明显*（*apparent*）。飞机晚点或者误机，或者在高速公路上错过了出口，都会让最精心设计的旅行变得复杂而混乱。下次如果你再被出乎意料的情况弄得*惊慌失措*（*disconcerted*），就可以用下面这些词来描述你的窘状。它们不能帮助你改善情况，但你至少可以用它们来抱怨。

apparent	intelligibility	patently
arrant	limpid	pellucid
clarity	lucidity	perceptible
conspicuous	manifest	perspicacity
discernible	obvious	ubiquitous
distinct	ostensibly	
evident	palpable	

abash	bewilderment	moil
addle	confounded	muddle
anarchy	derangement	perplexed
baffle	din	pother
bamboozle	discombobulated	welter
bedlam	disconcerted	

▶ **apparent**
/ə'pærənt/
a.

clearly seen; visible; not obscure or confusing 显而易见的，明白的

It was *apparent* that something was bothering Charles because his behavior was out of the ordinary. 查尔斯的行为很反常，显然在为某件事而困扰。

adverb: **apparently**

▶ **arrant**
/'ærənt/
a.

completely and thoroughly thus; it is what it is 彻头彻尾的，完全的

Louis's *arrant* feelings toward Celia prevented him from concentrating. 路易斯对西莉亚的感情投入过深使他无法集中注意力。

adverb: **arrantly**

▶ **clarity**
/'klærətɪ/
n.

clearness of thought, style, or appearance 清晰，清楚，明确

With sudden *clarity*, Sandra understood the calculus problem. 桑德拉恍然大悟，想通了这道微积分题。

▶ **conspicuous**
/kən'spɪkjʊəs/
a.

standing out; clearly exceptional or showy 显著的，引人注目的

Redheaded Timothy was *conspicuous* among the dark-haired Italians in the neighborhood. 左邻右舍都是黑发的意大利人，因此红发的蒂莫西特别引人注目。

adverb: **conspicuously**
noun: **conspicuousness**

▶ **discernible**
/dɪ's3·nəbl̩/
a.

clearly understandable through thought or vision 可辨别的，可识别的

Saturn was *discernible* in the southeastern night sky, even without a telescope. 夜空下，东南方的土星即使不用望远镜也可识别。

adverb: **discernibly**
verb: **discern**
noun: **discernment**

▶ **distinct**
/dɪ'stɪŋkt/
n.

clearly defined and recognizable; standing out from among its class 清晰可辨的；与……有所区别的

Jesse's *distinct* style of dressing made it easy to pick him out of the crowd. 杰西的另类装扮使他在人群中很显眼。

adverb: **distinctly**
adjective: **distinctive**

▶ **evident**
/'ɛvədənt/
a.

• worthy of notice; distinguishable 明显的；可辨识的

Because the reference book was so worn, it was *evident* that it was well-thumbed. 这本参考书很破旧，显然是被很多人翻阅过。

• apparent 显而易见的

Because Paul's hair had such an unusual sheen, it was *evident* that he was a swimmer. 保罗的头发有着与众不同的柔润光泽，显然他是个游泳爱好者。

adverb: **evidently**
noun: **evidence**

▶ **intelligibility** intellectual understanding; mental clarity 理解力
/ɪnˌtɛlɪdʒə'bɪlətɪ/
n.

The chimpanzee demonstrated such *intelligibility* in his responses to the scientists that it was difficult for them to remember that they were working with an animal and not a human. 在与科学家的互动中，黑猩猩表现出了很强的理解力，以致于科学家都忘了他们是在和动物而不是在和人类一起工作。

adjective: **intelligible**
adverb: **intelligibly**

▶ **limpid**
/ˈlɪmpɪd/
a.

clear and clean; without blemish or confusion 清澈的，干净的

Emily's *limpid* eyes said it all; she was truly in love with Clarence. 埃米莉水灵灵的眼睛说明了一切：她是真的爱上了克拉伦斯。

adverb: **limpidly**

▶ **lucidity**
/luˈsɪdətɪ/
n.

clearness of thought; capacity to perceive the thought 清楚；明白

Clarence, however, lacked the *lucidity* to recognize Emily's adoration. 然而，克拉伦斯却无法领会埃米莉的一片深情。

adverb: **lucidly**
adjective: **lucid**

▶ **manifest**
/ˈmænəˌfɛst/
v.

to show plainly; to reveal 显示，表明

He *manifested* his displeasure in his body language and tone of voice. 从肢体语言和说话语调上都可以看出他的不悦。

adverb: **manifestly**
adjective: **manifest**

▶ **obvious**
/ˈɑbvɪəs/

apparent; easily seen or seen through; without subterfuge 明显的，显而易见的；不加掩饰的

a. Laurel's *obvious* pleasure was apparent in her facial expression. 劳雷尔将快乐都写在脸上。

adverb: **obviously**
noun: **obviousness**

▶ **ostensibly**
/ɑs'tɛnsəblɪ/
ad.

seeming to mean something or to be interpreted as such 表面上

Although we were *ostensibly* invited because we were friends of the host, in reality, he was using our presence to enhance his political position in the community. 表面上，我们因为是主人的朋友而受到邀请，但实际上他想利用我们的到场来提升自己在社区的政治影响力。

adjective: **ostensible**

▶ **palpable**
/'pælpəbl̩/
a.

clear and discernible; noticeable by touch 清楚的，可觉察的；可触知的

The unease among the group members was *palpable* as they stared at their feet and cleared their throats. 从队员们低头盯着脚和清嗓子的动作就能看出他们很紧张。

adverb: **palpably**

▶ **patently**
/'petn̩tlɪ/
ad.

openly; plainly; clearly 明显地，显然地

It was *patently* clear from the reaction of the jury that the defense attorney had the upper hand. 从陪审团的反应可明显看出辩方律师占上风。

The lackadaisical behavior of the seniors *patently* indicated their seniorities. 上司们懒洋洋的姿态摆明着他们年长资深。

adjective: **patent**

► **pellucid**
/pəˈlusɪd/

a.

clear in style, manner, or appearance 清晰的，明白的

Her *pellucid* attempts to impress the young man were useless since he was more interested in watching the football game. 她决意要引起那个年轻人的注意，但未奏效，因为他对看足球赛更感兴趣。

adverb: **pellucidly**

► **perceptible**
/pɚˈsɛptəbl̩/

a.

capable of being perceived by the senses or the intellect 可感觉到的，可感知的

The change in atmospheric pressure was *perceptible* to me as soon as I felt a headache developing. 我只要一开始头疼就知道气压发生了变化。

noun: **perception**
adverb: **perceptively**

► **perspicacity**
/pɝˈspɪˈkæsəti/

n.

acuteness of perception and understanding 睿智，明察是非

The five-year-old's *perspicacity* amazed all who heard him answer the question. 这个五岁小孩的机敏和睿智令所有听到他回答问题的人震惊。

adjective: **perspicacious**
adverb: **perspicaciously**

► **ubiquitous**
/juˈbɪkwətəs/

a.

all over; always present and noticeable 无处不在的，普遍存在的

The new principal was *ubiquitous* that fall; he went out of his way to show students that he cared and that he was always around if they needed him. 那年秋天这位新校长的

身影随处可见，他不辞辛苦旨在让学生们明白他的用心，让需要他帮助的学生随时都可以找到他。

adverb: **ubiquitously**
noun: **ubiquity**

· ·

▶ **abash**
/ə'bæʃ/
v.

to confuse or distress; to cause perplexity and uncertainty
使……受羞辱

He *abashed* his opponent by unearthing a past embarrassing incident that few people knew about. 他揭露了对手一件鲜为人知的丑闻，达到了羞辱他的目的。

adjective: **abashed**
adverb: **abashedly**

▶ **addle**
/'ædl/
v.

cause to become unclear or confusing 使……混乱，使……迷惑

Rene *addled* the frail, old librarian by being rude and indifferent to the man's senior position and personal feelings. 勒内对这位年老力衰的图书管理员蛮横无礼，全然不顾其长辈身份和个人感受，结果把图书管理员气晕了。

adjective: **addled**

▶ **anarchy**
/'ænɚkɪ/
n.

• confusion and disruption; without clearness in mind or purpose 混乱

Once the teacher left the room, all order fell apart and the students resorted to total *anarchy*. 一旦老师一离开教室，一切秩序荡然无存，学生们就会闹成一片。

• government without a designated leader 无政府状态

After the overthrow of the king, *anarchy* ruled throughout the country. 国王被推翻后，整个国家陷入了无政府状态。

▶ **baffle**
/ˈbæfḷ/
v.

to confuse; to forestall action or understanding 使困惑，使为难

The prosecution lawyer tried to *baffle* the witness with his cleverness, but the witness was too smart and would not be dissuaded from her testimony. 检察官试图凭借聪明才智为难证人，但技高一筹的证人并未听从劝阻而拒绝作证。

adjective: **baffled**
noun: **bafflement**

▶ **bamboozle**
/bæmˈbuzḷ/
v.

to trick and confuse 欺骗，愚弄，蒙蔽

The wily student's attempt to *bamboozle* the counselor with double-talk did not work, and he was promptly sent back to class. 这个自作聪明的学生对辅导员含糊其辞，试图愚弄辅导员，可未能如愿，他马上被送回了教室。

adjective: **bamboozled**

▶ **bedlam**
/ˈbɛdləm/
n.

• a place of noisy uproar and confusion 吵闹嘈杂的地方

When the substitute teacher arrived, she found the classroom in a state of *bedlam* and it took her the remainder of the hour to restore order. 代课教师到达时发现教室里一片嘈杂。她花了所有剩余的时间来维持秩序。

• an insane asylum (old-fashioned term) [旧]精神病院，疯人院

In the Victorian era in England, mental patients were confined to *bedlam*. 维多利亚时代的英国，精神病患者都被关在精神病院里。

► **bewilderment** state of being confused, perplexed, and/or disoriented 迷惑，
/bɪˈwɪldəˌmənt/ 混乱
n.

> Hansel and Gretel's **bewilderment** was so obvious that it did not take the witch long to coerce them into her home. 汉塞尔和格蕾特尔明显神志不清了，女巫并没花多久就把他们引到了她家。

> verb: **bewilder**
> adjective: **bewildered**

► **confounded** confused or stunned; totally perplexed 困惑的，不知所
/kənˈfaʊndɪd/ 措的
a.

> Patricia was **confounded** by her boss's change of heart when he granted her extra vacation over the holidays so that she could visit her family in New Mexico. 老板改变了主意，批准帕特里夏延长假期去新墨西哥看望家人，弄得帕特里夏有点摸不着头脑。

> adverb: **confoundedly**
> verb: **confound**

► **derangement** disturbance or disorderliness; maximum confusion to the
/dɪˈrendʒmənt/ point of mental instability 混乱
n.

> There was such a **derangement** in the classroom that the teacher thought she would surely lose her mind before the end of the semester. 课堂秩序如此混乱，使身为老师的她觉得自己在学期结束前肯定会疯掉。

> adjective: **deranged**

► **din** loud noise or confusion, usually from a crowd 喧闹，嘈杂
/dɪn/

n. Often, indoor stadiums are poorly equipped to handle noise so that the *din* can be overwhelming for the crowds who come to view the games. 体育馆通常很少配备减噪装置，这使得观众常常为巨大的噪音所扰。

▶**discombobulated** confused and taken off guard by circumstances 困惑
/dɪskəm'bɑbjəˌletɪd/ 的，慌乱不安的
a.

My cousin became so *discombobulated* by the accident that her usually calm demeanor was no longer in evidence. 事故使堂妹非常慌乱不安，言谈举止间失去了往日的镇静。

verb: **discombobulate**
noun: **discombobulation**

▶**disconcerted** upset; confused; put off balance 不安的
/ˌdɪskən'sɝtɪd/
a. My grandmother was so *disconcerted* by the news that she was unable to speak for several minutes. 看到新闻时祖母异常不安，几分钟都说不出话。

adverb: **disconcertedly**
verb: **disconcert**

▶**moil** a situation that is confused, in a turmoil, and/or uncertain
/mɔɪl/ 混乱的状态，不确定的状态
n.

Patrick William found himself in such a *moil* that he thought he would never be able to save himself. 帕特里克·威廉发觉自己已陷入了无法自拔的混乱中。

▶**muddle** to think, act, or proceed in a confused or aimless manner 糊
/'mʌdl̩/ 涂地过日子，瞎混
v.

Not clear about exactly what was expected of him on the new job, Giorgio *muddled* along until somebody gave him specific directions. 由于不清楚新的工作要他做什么，在被告知明确的要求之前，乔治一直在混日子，

adjective: **muddled**

▶**perplexed**
/pɚˈplɛkst/
a.

confused, or bewildered 困惑的，糊涂的

Wilma was ***perplexed*** by the disappearance of her glasses and didn't realize they were on the top of her head. 威尔马很疑惑她的眼镜去哪儿了，却没意识到就在自己头上。

verb: **perplex**
noun: **perplexity**

▶**pother**
/ˈpɑðɚ/
n.

a commotion or a disturbance; a state of nervous activity 混乱，骚动；紧张不安

My little sister was in such a ***pother*** about her impending piano recital that I was concerned that she would forget how to play her piece. 日益迫近的钢琴独奏会使妹妹紧张不安，我真担心她会忘记自己的曲目。

▶**welter**
/ˈwɛltɚ/
n.

a confused mass; a jumble; total disorganization and perplexity 混乱，一团糟，杂乱无章

The poorly organized field trip was a ***welter*** of miscommunication and disgruntled children. 这次郊游组织得很不好，孩子们沟通不足，个个快快不快，结果弄得一团糟。

Sentence Completion 完成句子

Circle the word or word pair that best completes the meaning of the sentence. 圈出最符合句子含义的词或一对词。

1. Visibility was so poor that the headlights of the oncoming car were barely _____ in the fog.
   A. conspicuous
   B. arrant
   C. discernible
   D. obvious
   E. manifest

2. Martha's wild story was so _____ a lie that I couldn't believe the teacher was falling for it.
   A. ostensibly
   B. patently
   C. intelligibly
   D. limpidly
   E. palpably

3. Drew's _____ was so _____ that the calculus teacher went over the problem once again.
   A. lucidity/evident
   B. clarity/manifest
   C. bafflement/addled
   D. perplexity/apparent
   E. derangement/discombobulated

4. Ryan's messy desk was such a _____ of papers and
files that it was _____ he would never find the sheet of
figures he was looking for.
A. din/confounded
B. bewilderment/discernible
C. intelligibility/palpable
D. muddle/obvious
E. pother/conspicuous

5. There was such a _____ in the classroom that the
substitute teacher became totally _____.
A. din/discombobulated
B. derangement/ostensive
C. bedlam/limpid
D. clarity/intelligible
E. bafflement/confounded

Quick Matching 快速配对

*Write the letter of the definition shown in the right column next
to the word that matches it in the left column.* 在右栏中找出与
左栏单词相符的定义，将对应的字母写在单词旁。

_____1. disconcerted	A. clearly defined and recognizable
_____2. muddled	B. confused and causing uncertainty and embarrassment
_____3. abashed	C. standing out from the rest
_____4. conspicuous	D. seeming to act aimlessly, without reason
_____5. distinct	E. confused and thrown off balance mentally

Complete the Story 完成故事

Using these words selected from this unit, fill in the blanks to complete the story. 用本单元的词汇填空，完成故事。

bewilderment	perplexing
perceptible	discernible
muddled	evidently
apparent	baffle
perspicacity	lucidity
evidence	confounded
moil	

Mystery stories have ＿＿＿＿＿ gained a conspicuous place in the hearts of reading or viewing audiences. Some mysteries have clearly ＿＿＿＿＿ story lines and easily ＿＿＿＿＿ clues; they do not ＿＿＿＿＿ the audience with ＿＿＿＿＿ plots or unusual characters. In contrast, some mysteries are so ＿＿＿＿＿ that the viewer/reader is uncertain of the truth until the last moment. These plots are often ＿＿＿＿＿ with unusual twists, and the action is in such a ＿＿＿＿＿ that one finds it difficult to figure out what is going on.

Main characters in mysteries are a big part of the stories' success. Sometimes these are unique personalities, such as the old television cop Columbo or Agatha Christie's Hercule Poirot. These characters often act ＿＿＿＿＿ and confused about what is going on, while actually they are cleverly getting to the bottom of the problem. Their supposed ＿＿＿＿＿ is their strongest weapon. Other mystery solvers, such as Sherlock Holmes, are known for their fine intelligence and steel-trap

memories. No _____ is ever overlooked, and they tackle
each mystery with _____ and _____. Over the
years countless mysteries and mystery characters have been
introduced to the reading and viewing public.

ANSWERS 答案
Sentence Completion 完成句子：1-C, 2-B, 3-D, 4-D, 5-A
Quick Matching 快速配对：1-E, 2-D, 3-B, 4-C, 5-A
Complete the Story 完成故事：evidently, perceptible,
discernible, baffle, perplexing, unapparent, confounded,
moil, muddled, bewilderment, evidence, lucidity,
perspicacity

Review 1 复习 1

These sentences include words from the previous four units. 下列句子需要使用前面四个单元的词汇。

Sentence Completion 完成句子

Circle the word pair that best completes the meaning of the sentence. 圈出最符合句子含义的一对词。

1. The busy mother of three-year-old triplets was enjoying a _____ moment of quiet in contrast to the usual, _____ noise of living with three toddlers.

   A. obvious/fleeting

   B. rarefied/unremitting

   C. periodic/perpetual

   D. genuine/incidental

   E. conspicuous/sporadic

2. The injured passenger was barely _____; he stared at the young female police officer with _____ clearly showing on his face.

   A. apparent/irrelevance

   B. resistant/insistence

   C. coherent/perplexity

   D. lucid/perceptibility

   E. noteworthy/veracity

3. When you write a composition, you want to edit out all
_____ words because most people prefer to read
something that has _____ and conciseness.
A. inconsequential/clarity
B. discernible/legitimacy
C. applicable/extraneous
D. immaterial/semblance
E. contingent/illusion

4. The warm front was only _____; we were living near
the Canadian border, and it was (a) _____ to think that
winter would be over in late February.
A. short-lived/momentous
B. imaginative/legitimate
C. fleeting/abstruse
D. indefatigable/pother
E. transitory/fantasy

5. It is important that senior citizens have _____ checkups
with their doctors in order to rule out the possibilities of their
having developed _____ diseases such as diabetes.
A. contingent/momentous
B. valid/inconsequential
C. periodic/chronic
D. authentic/erroneous
E. portentous/short-lived

ANSWERS 答案
1-B, 2-C, 3-A, 4-E, 5-C

SECTION II

Unit 1 **Beauty and the Beast** 美女与野兽 ▶ alluring, appealing, beaming, comely, dazzling, exquisite, gorgeous, luminous, lustrous, pulchritude, radiant, ravishing, resplendent, salacious, scintillate, striking ▶ barbarian, bestial, boorish, brutish, churlish, coarse, crass, depraved, feral, gross, ill-bred, loutish, Neanderthal, oafish, rude, uncouth, vulgar

Unit 2 **Smart As a Tack or Dumber Than Dirt** 聪明如钉子还是沉默赛泥土 ▶ acumen, acute, astute, canny, discernment, judicious, keenness, perceptive, perspicacity, politic, prudent, sagacity, sapience, shrewd ▶ buffoon, fatuous, folly, imprudent, inadvisable, inane, indiscreet, inexpedient, injudicious, ludicrous, preposterous, rash, witless

Unit 3 **Roar Like a Lion or Mew Like a Kitten** 狮子般怒吼还是猫咪般喵呜 ▶ assuage, appease, composed, détente, dormant, imperturbable, levelheaded, mitigate, placate, placid, quiescent, repose, serene, slack, sluggish, tranquility ▶ blatant, boisterous, brattle, brawl, clamorous, din, discordant, fractious, hubbub, obstreperous, ostentatious, strident, truculent, turbulent, vociferous

Unit 4 **Something Old, Something New** 一些陈旧，一些新颖 ▶ budding, burgeoning, embryonic, fledgling, incipient, initiate, innovation, naive, nascent, neophyte, neoteric, postulant, proselyte, raw, rudimentary, shaver, stripling, untried ▶ antediluvian, antiquated, archaic, dateless, fossilized, full-fledged, geriatric, gerontic, hoary, obsolescence, outmoded, passé, prehistoric, primeval, primitive, primordial, seasoned, superannuated, venerable, veteran

Beauty and the Beast
美女与野兽

我们有无数描述美丽与可爱的词汇。只需花一会儿工夫翻看一下当代的女性杂志《魅力》（*Glamour*）或者《时尚》（*Vogue*），学习一下各种装扮自己的方法，读者便可以变得更加美丽（*gorgeous*）、更加容光焕发（*radiant*），甚至具有*不可抗拒的*（*irresistible*）魅力。

　　不幸的是，每朵玫瑰都有刺，而且这刺可能是*很难对付的*（*churlish*）、粗糙的（*crass*）甚至*邪恶的*（*depraved*），企图摧毁一切可爱而美丽的事物。无论如何，下面列出了很多单词，你可以用它们来描述美好的和丑恶的事物。

alluring	gorgeous	resplendent
appealing	luminous	salacious
beaming	lustrous	scintillate
comely	pulchritude	striking
dazzling	radiant	
exquisite	ravishing	

barbarian	crass	Neanderthal
bestial	depraved	oafish
boorish	feral	rude
brutish	gross	uncouth
churlish	ill-bred	vulgar
coarse	loutish	

▶**alluring**
/əˈlʊrɪŋ/
a.

highly, often subtly attractive 有诱惑力的

In her early years, Katharine Hepburn was considered an *alluring* star. 出道早期，凯瑟琳·赫本被认为是极具魅力的明星。

verb: **allure**
adverb: **alluringly**

▶**appealing**
/əˈpilɪŋ/
a.

attractive and inviting 有吸引力的

The job was very *appealing*; the hours and the tasks seemed totally suited to me. 这份工作太有吸引力了，从工作时间到工作内容都完全符合我的意愿。

verb: **appeal**
adverb: **appealingly**

▶**beaming**
/bimɪŋ/
a.

the state of being radiant; showing pleasure and happiness; shining 发光的；眉开眼笑的

My grandmother's *beaming* smile assured me that I had chosen the right birthday present for her. 祖母脸上洋溢着笑容，看来我的确选对了生日礼物。

noun: **beam**
verb: **beam**

▶**comely**
/ˈkʌmlɪ/
a.

wholesome in appearance; attractively pleasing in looks and/or behavior 标致的，好看的

Moira was a *comely* young woman; the men in the village were in awe of her good looks. 莫伊拉年轻漂亮。她的美貌让村里的男人们折服。

noun: **comeliness**

▶**dazzling**
/ˈdæzl̩ɪŋ/
a.

blinding in extravagance or beauty; amazing and over-whelming 炫目的，眼花缭乱的

Her rhinestone-studded, shimmery gown enhanced Natalie's *dazzling* entrance to the party. 这件镶嵌着人造钻石而无比闪耀的礼服使得纳塔利在聚会上的出现格外夺目。

verb: **dazzle**
noun: **dazzler**

▶**exquisite**
/ˈɛkskwɪzɪt/
a.

characterized by unusual and often intricate beauty or design; intense; keen 精美的，制作精良的

Clara's new engagement ring was an *exquisite* two-carat diamond in an unusual setting. 克拉拉的新订婚戒指是一枚两克拉不规则镶嵌且制作精美的钻戒。

noun: **exquisiteness**
adverb: **exquisitely**

▶**gorgeous**
/ˈgɔrdʒəs/
a.

dazzlingly beautiful or magnificent; (less formal) wonderful, even delightful 非常漂亮的，华美的；(非正式)极好的，称心的

Because of the atmospheric conditions, the evening's sunset was *gorgeous*. 由于大气环境的原因，今晚的日落景色异常华美。

noun: **gorgeousness**
adverb: **gorgeously**

▶**luminous**
/ˈlumənəs/
a.

• having to do with light or emitting light 发光的，有光泽的

Henrietta's skin was *luminous* in the candlelight. 亨丽埃塔的皮肤在烛光映衬下显得很有光泽。

- seeming to be glowing with beauty 魅力四射的

The model's *luminous* beauty was evident through all of her stage makeup. 这个浓妆艳抹的模特在舞台上魅力四射。

noun: **luminosity**
adverb: **luminously**
verb: **illuminate**

▶ **lustrous**
/ˈlʌstrəs/
a.

brilliant; lovely; outstandingly glowing and unusual 有光泽的

Her long, freshly washed hair was *lustrous*. 她刚洗的长发很有光泽。

adverb: **lustrously**
noun: **lustrousness**

▶ **pulchritude**
/ˈpʌlkrɪˌtjud/
n.

extreme beauty and unusual appeal （尤指女性的）美貌

The *pulchritude* of the young starlet overwhelmed the audience when she stepped onto the stage. 当这位年轻演员登上舞台的时候，观众们都为她的美貌而折服。

adjective: **pulchritudinous**

▶ **radiant**
/ˈredɪənt/
a.

- emitting heat, light, or radiation 辐射放热的

The room was kept warm by *radiant* heat. 屋子里靠辐射热取暖。

- beaming; overwhelmed by pleasure or extreme beauty 有魅力的，容光焕发的

Her beauty was enhanced by her *radiant* smile. 热情洋溢的笑容使她更具魅力。

adverb: **radiantly**

noun: **radiance**

▶ **ravishing**
/'rævɪʃɪŋ/
a.

extremely attractive; entrancing 非常美丽的；令人陶醉的

Without a doubt the young woman was a *ravishing* beauty. 无疑，这个年轻女郎非常漂亮。

adverb: **ravishingly**

noun: **ravishment**

▶ **resplendent**
/rɪ'splɛndənt/
a.

splendid or dazzling in appearance; brilliant 辉煌的，华丽的，令人眩目的

The groom was *resplendent* in his tuxedo and ruffled, formal shirt. 穿着正式的无尾礼服以及褶饰衬衣，新郎看上去帅极了。

adverb: **resplendently**

▶ **salacious**
/sə'leʃəs/
a.

appealing, especially in a sexual or even lewd manner 好色的，淫荡的

The stranger's *salacious* glance made it clear just what his intentions were. 这个陌生人好色的眼神完全暴露了他的内心想法。

noun: **salaciousness**

adverb: **salaciously**

▶ **scintillate**
/'sɪntl̩et/
v.

to sparkle or shine, even to send off sparks or flashes 闪耀光芒，才华横溢

The boring professor gave a far from *scintillating* lecture. 这个教授的讲座平淡无奇，令人乏味。

adjective: **scintillating**
adverb: **scintillatingly**

▶ **striking**
/ˈstraɪkɪŋ/
a.

extremely noticeable; outstandingly attractive or significant 显著的，引人注目的

Because the model was very dark and nearly 6 feet tall, she was a very *striking* woman. 这个女模特皮肤黝黑，身高将近6英尺，十分引人注目。

adverb: **strikingly**

....

▶ **barbarian**
/bɑrˈbɛrɪən/
n.

a fierce, insensitive, cruel, or uncultured person 野蛮人，粗野的人

Bruce was so unsophisticated that his behavior was like a *barbarian*. During the formal dinner, he ate his entire meal with his spoon, and he chewed with his mouth open. 布鲁斯是如此没有教养，就像未开化的野蛮人一样。在正式晚宴上，他全部用汤勺进餐，咀嚼时也不闭上嘴巴。

The *barbarians* waged war upon those who were trying to civilize them. 那些野蛮人对试图教化他们的人发起了战争。

noun: **barbarianism**
adjective: **barbarian, barbaric**

▶ **bestial**
/ˈbɛstʃəl/
a.

marked by brutality; lacking reason or humanity; depraved and beastly 残忍的

The soldiers were accused of *bestial* acts against unarmed civilians. 士兵对手无寸铁的平民的残忍行径遭到人们的谴责。

noun: **bestiality**
adverb: **bestially**

▶ **boorish**
/'burɪʃ/
a.

rude and clumsy; lacking polish, courtesy, or humanity 粗鲁的

Raymond's character had become so *boorish* that his friends stopped asking him to go anywhere with them because he embarrassed them. 雷蒙德变得越来越粗鲁，朋友们都不再邀请他一同出行以免自取其辱。

noun: **boor**
adverb: **boorishly**

▶ **brutish**
/'brutɪʃ/
a.

crude in feeling; coarse; rough; uncivilized 兽性的

The character Hannibal Lector had to be totally restrained because of his *brutish*, cannibalistic actions. 汉尼拔·莱克特这一角色因其残忍的兽行和食人肉行为而必须被完全监禁。

noun: **brute**
adverb: **brutishly**

▶ **churlish**
/'tʃɜlɪʃ/
a.

boorish; vulgar; of a dark nature; uncouth and uncivilized 无礼的

When the young man's attitude became *churlish*, he was quickly reprimanded by his father. 这个年轻人的态度变得粗暴无礼，没多久就挨了父亲的骂。

noun: **churl**
adverb: **churlishly**

▶ **coarse**
/kors/
a.

rough; uncouth; not very civilized or polished 粗糙的；粗鲁的

The uneducated mountain man had a *coarse* way about him, but under it all he was very gentle. 这个未受教育的山里人尽管粗鲁，但内心却十分善良。

noun: **coarseness**

adverb: **coarsely**

▶ **crass**
/kræs/
a.

crude; unrefined; lacking sensibility 粗鲁的；全然不顾他人的

Despite his rather *crass* mannerisms, he had a tender heart and an understanding way about him. 尽管他举止粗鲁，但内心却温柔体贴、善解人意。

noun: **crassness**

adverb: **crassly**

▶ **depraved**
/dɪ'prevd/
a.

morally corrupt; morally unconventional, even perverted 堕落的，道德败坏的

Many of the inmates in that part of the prison are *depraved* people, which is often a result of their dysfunctional upbringings. 很多关押在这片监狱里的犯人都是道德败坏之徒，这通常与从小未受过正当教育有关。

verb: **deprave**

adverb: **depravedly**

noun: **depravity**

▶ **feral**
/'fɪrəl/
a.

untamed, uncouth, and uncivilized; suggestive of an animal state of existence （动物）兽性的

Although we thought we had domesticated the wolfhound, when he smelled blood, he turned *feral* and started growling and gnashing his teeth. 尽管我们以为这只狼狗被驯化了，可当他嗅到血腥味时马上就恢复了兽性，开始嗥叫并磨牙。

▶ **gross**
/gros/

offensive; disgusting; without sensitivity or sophistication 粗鲁的，不雅的；缺乏敏感的

a.　The crime scene was incredibly *gross*; everyone was relieved when the lieutenant said the investigation would be suspended until daylight. 犯罪现场惨不忍睹。当中尉说调查将暂缓到次日白天再进行时，所有人都松了口气。

noun: **grossness**
adverb: **grossly**

▶ **ill-bred**
/ˌɪl'brɛd/
a.

poorly brought up; impolite; unpolished; crude 无教养的，粗鲁的

Because she had no parents and had grown up largely on her own, Tana was *ill-bred*, but she learned quickly in her new home because she didn't want to upset anyone. 塔娜从小无父无母，基本上是自己养活自己，所以缺乏教养。但她在新家里学东西很快，因为她不愿烦扰任何人。

▶ **loutish**
/'laʊtɪʃ/
a.

having characteristics of an awkward or stupid person （人）笨拙的，愚蠢的

Although her actions were occasionally *loutish*, Kristie became more and more adept in social situations. 尽管克里斯蒂偶尔行动迟缓，可她对现实状况的处理却越来越在行。

noun: **loutishness, lout**
adverb: **loutishly**

▶ **Neanderthal**
/nɪ'ændəˌtɑl/
n., a.

noun: an extinct human species; early Homo sapien 尼安德特人（石器时代住在欧洲的原始人）

Anthropologists have found much evidence of *Neanderthal* man in the region of Dusseldorf, Germany. 考古学家在德国的杜塞尔多夫地区发现了许多尼安德特人存在的证据。

adjective: crude, boorish, or awkward 粗野的

Some bachelors live such crude and basic lives that women view them as *Neanderthals*. 一些过着简单而粗俗生活的单身汉被女人们视为粗野的人。

▶**oafish**
/'ofɪʃ/
a.

clumsy, stupid, crude, or awkward in behavior or demeanor 笨拙的

At 6 feet 6 inches, Larry was often *oafish* in a small space, but on a basketball court he was poetry in motion: 拉里6.6英尺的身高使他在小空间中经常显得很笨拙，可到了篮球场上，他的动作则异常优美。

noun: **oaf**
adverb: **oafishly**

▶**rude**
/rud/
a.

• relatively undeveloped or primitive 简陋的，粗制的

The furniture was *rude* in its design, reflecting that specialized tools were not used when it was built. 这个家具设计简陋粗糙，说明制作时没有使用特殊工具。

• ill-mannered and discourteous 不礼貌的，粗鲁的

The child's *rude* behavior suggested that his parents were inadequate role models for behavior and decorum. 这个孩子行为粗鲁，说明父母在行为及礼仪上没有起到足够的示范作用。

noun: **rudeness**
adverb: **rudely**

▶**uncouth**
/ʌn'kuθ/
a.

crude and unrefined; awkward, clumsy, and/or ungraceful 粗野的；笨拙的，不优雅的

The basketball player's *uncouth* behavior got him thrown out of the game. 篮球运动员的粗野行为导致他被罚出局。

noun: **uncouthness**
adverb: **uncouthly**

▶ **vulgar**
/ˈvʌlgɚ/
a.

common and ordinary; unrefined and unpolished 平庸的；粗俗的，粗野的

The child's *vulgar* language surprised his grandmother; she couldn't believe he would use such language in front of her. 孩子粗俗的语言使他祖母很吃惊；她不敢相信孩子会当着自己的面说出这样的话。

noun: **vulgarity**
adverb: **vulgarly**

Sentence Completion 完成句子

Circle the word or word pair that best completes the meaning of the sentence. 圈出最符合句子含义的词或一对词。

1. The auburn-haired model had _____ skin that seemed to glow from within.
   A. luminous
   B. comely
   C. beaming
   D. dazzling
   E. appealing

2. The diamonds on display at the jewelry store were _____ in their gleam and glimmer; I was overwhelmed by their purity.
   A. lustrous
   B. appealing
   C. striking
   D. salacious
   E. radiant

3. Monica's most _____ feature is her _____ smile.
   A. striking/beaming
   B. churlish/comely
   C. gorgeous/brutish
   D. feral/oafish
   E. scintillating/rude

4. Today, most expensive shampoos guarantee _____
   hair and a _____ shine.
   A. luminous/coarse
   B. radiant/lustrous
   C. comely/scintillating
   D. vulgar/uncouth
   E. ravishing/ill-bred

5. The morally _____ creature was so crude and untamed
   that his actions indicated _____ behavior.
   A. appealing/oafish
   B. striking/barbarian
   C. crass/coarse
   D. churlish/boorish
   E. depraved/feral

Quick Matching 快速配对

Write the letter of the definition shown in the right column next to the word that matches it in the left column. 在右栏中找出与左栏单词相符的定义，将对应的字母写在单词旁。

_____1. Neanderthal   A. entrancing and attractive

_____2. bestial   B. crude and unrefined

_____3. crass   C. sparkling with energy

_____4. scintillating   D. marked by brutality; lacking
                                humanity

_____5. ravishing   E. possessing prehistoric behavior

Complete the Story 完成故事

Using these words selected from this unit, fill in the blanks to complete the story. 用本单元的词汇填空，完成故事。

vulgar	gorgeous
reprehensible	exquisite
appeal	boors
ill-bred	salacious
dazzling	rude
oafish	depraved
lustrous	comely
beaming	feral
coarse	pulchritude
resplendent	

Children's fairy and folk tales are often more extreme than contemporary Golden Book and Disney presentations might indicate. Grimm's *Fairy Tales*, for instance, were often dark and somewhat _____ tales with _____ characters who were frequently uncivilized _____ identified by their _____ behavior and/or actions. Some of the "bad characters" are even _____ beasts who prey on the innocent, such as the wolf in "Little Red Riding Hood." The little girl in "The Red Shoes" had to have her feet removed to free her of the curse of the shoes!

In contrast to such _____ characters and _____ behavior are the "good characters" whose _____ is sometimes so extreme that their _____ becomes _____. The story of Cinderella, for instance, found in many cultures, is a _____ lass who must slave under the jealous eye of her _____ stepsisters and _____ stepmother. Nevertheless, when the magic moment arrives, this girl turns into an _____ princess, _____ in gown and tiara, with _____ hair, _____ skin, a _____ smile, and a jubilant, _____ prince ready to do her bidding.

ANSWERS 答案

Sentence Completion 完成句子: 1-A, 2-E, 3-A, 4-B, 5-E

Quick Matching 快速配对: 1-E, 2-D, 3-B, 4-C, 5-A

Complete the Story 完成故事: depraved, reprehensible, boors, coarse, feral, vulgar, rude, pulchritude, appeal, salacious, comely, oafish, ill-bred, exquisite, resplendent, lustrous, gorgeous, dazzling, beaming

Smart As a Tack or Dumber Than Dirt
聪明如钉子还是沉默赛泥土

你有没有留意过，电视情景喜剧中的主要角色一般都是两种类型？要么他们是*鲁莽的小丑*（*imprudent buffoons*），常因草率*的*（*rash*）或者*愚蠢的*（*witless*）想法导致*滑稽的*（*ludicrous*）行为和*轻率的*（*injudicious*）决定；要么他们都是些聪明角色，对生活的看法*敏锐*（*keen*）且*洞察力强*（*perceptive*），总是有一些*独到的见解*（*politic discernment*）。他们极为*睿智*（*sagacity*）会让你觉得难以置信。

电视情景喜剧很少有性格较为平和或者"正常的"、比较有深度的角色。我们看到的角色性格都过于极端，很不现实。你无法对电视里的人物做些什么，但至少你可以掌握一些词汇，用来描述和区别这些人物。

acumen	judicious	prudent
acute	keenness	sagacity
astute	perceptive	sapience
canny	perspicacity	shrewd
discernment	politic	

. . . .

buffoon	inane	preposterous
fatuous	indiscreet	rash
folly	inexpedient	witless
imprudent	injudicious	
inadvisable	ludicrous	

▶ **acumen**
/ə'kjumən/
n.

keenness of mind; good insight; quickness; accuracy 聪明；敏锐；快速；准确

Fatima's mathematical *acumen* was so sharp that she did not find her calculus class difficult at all. 法蒂玛对数学悟性极高，她从不觉得微积分课有什么难的。

▶ **acute**
/ə'kjut/
a.

clever; sharp of mind; incisive 聪明的；灵敏的，敏锐的

Her mother's hearing was so *acute* that Martha was usually caught when she tried to sneak in after curfew. 玛莎母亲的听觉太敏锐了，通常只要她试图在宵禁后偷偷溜进来都会被发觉。

adverb: **acutely**
noun: **acuteness**

▶ **astute**
/ə'stut/
a.

clever and insightful; having an innate ability to understand or perceive 聪明的；有眼光的；精明的，敏锐的

The grandmother had *astute* intuition so she knew exactly when her grandchildren had done something wrong. 祖母的直觉很敏锐。只要孙儿们做错事了，她都能觉察出来。

noun: **astuteness**
adverb: **astutely**

▶ **canny**
/'kænɪ/
a.

careful; shrewd; clever; wily; full of guile 精明的，不易上当的

Because Robert was so *canny*, no one could get away with anything when he was around. 罗伯特十分精明，和他打交道，没有人能占到便宜。

noun: **canniness**
adverb: **cannily**

verb: **perceive**
adverb: **perceptively**

▶ **perspicacity** acuteness of perception, discernment, or understanding 敏锐，
/pɜˈspɪˈkæsətɪ/ 睿智
n.

Sara's *perspicacity* enabled her to solve the problem before anyone else. 萨拉的聪明才智使她最先攻克了这道难题。

adjective: **perspicacious**
adverb: **perspicaciously**

▶ **politic** prudent, expedient, and shrewd and artful 慎重的，精明
/ˈpɑləˌtɪk/ 的，深谋远虑的
a.

Being *politic* as usual, Gracie was careful not to lose her temper even though the situation had angered her greatly. 尽管这事情让她很恼火，但格雷西仍然像往常一样慎重，很小心地克制着自己的脾气。

adverb: **politicly**

▶ **prudent** wise and careful; economical and exercising good judgment
/ˈprudn̩t/ 慎重的；精打细算的
a.

Muhammad was *prudent* with his allowance; he spent just enough to cover his basic needs. 穆罕默德对开销总是精打细算的，只会买一些生活必需品。

noun: **prudence, prude**
adverb: **prudently**

▶ ˈgacity the quality of being discerning, sound in judgment,
ˈgæsətɪ/ and farsighted; wisdom 睿智，精明

Officer Eugene's *sagacity* was amazing; he was easily

▶ **discernment** keenness of insight and judgment 识别能力，洞察力
/dɪ'sɜ·nmənt/

n.
Sammy solved the problem using insight and *discernment*.
萨米凭借敏锐的洞察力解决了这个问题。

verb: **discern**
adjective: **discerning**

▶ **judicious** having sound and prudent judgment 明智的，能作合情
/dʒu'dɪʃəs/ 合理判断的

a.
The older lawyer was *judicious* in his advice to the young
legal intern. 年长一些的律师给年轻的实习律师提出了合
理的建议。

adjective (alternative): **judicial**
adverb: **judiciously**

▶ **keenness** smartly cutting or marked by remarkable mental quickness
/'kinnɪs/ understanding 睿智

n.
Anthony displayed such mental *keenness* that his f
always turned to him in times of distress. 安东尼很
因此朋友们只要一有麻烦就会去找他。

adverb: **keenly**
adjective: **keen**

▶ **perceptive** having a keen sense of understanding and di
/pɚ'sɛptɪv/ 灵敏的，有洞察力的

a.
Mr. Johnson is a *perceptive* teacher; h
when one of his students is strug
problems. 约翰逊先生是位很有洞察
他的学生面临难题，他都能觉察！

▶ **s**
/s
n.

able to figure out what was going on before the rest of the security squad had even assembled. 尤金警官有着惊人的觉察力，保安队尚未集合完毕，他就能猜出发生了什么事情。

noun: **sagacious**
adverb: **sagaciously**
adjective: **sage**

▶ **sapience**
/ˈsepɪəns/
n.

unusual intelligence and extraordinary discernment 智慧，贤明

George's *sapience* made him a natural for the detailed intelligence work required by his government. 乔治机敏过人，自然能胜任政府繁复的情报工作。

adjective: **sapient**
adverb: **sapiently**

▶ **shrewd**
/ʃrud/
a.

characterized by being cunning, sharply intelligent, and even tricky or calculating 敏捷的，精明的

Our Siamese cat is a *shrewd* animal; she holds perfectly still until the squirrels forget she's there. Then she pounces. 我们的暹罗猫非常精，她会一动不动直到松鼠忘记它存在时猛扑过去。

noun: **shrewdness**
adverb: **shrewdly**

....

▶ **buffoon**
/bəˈfun/
n.

a person given to clownish or foolish behavior; someone who is ludicrous and behaves stupidly 丑角；粗俗而愚蠢的人

The security person was such a *buffoon* that the intruders easily convinced him of their legitimacy and managed to burglarize all the offices. 保安愚蠢到很轻易就相信了来者的合法身份，使他们成功盗取了所有办公室的财物。

noun: **buffoonery**

▶ **fatuous**
/ˈfætʃʊəs/
a.

smugly and seemingly unconsciously foolish; delusive; prone to impossible speculation 愚昧的，昏庸的

Eloise was ***fatuous*** and believed that by dyeing her white hair red she could regain the beauty and sparkle of her youth. 埃洛伊丝愚昧之至以为只要把白发染红就能重拾青春美貌。

noun: **fatuousness**
adverb: **fatuously**

▶ **folly**
/ˈfɑlɪ/
n.

a lack of good sense or foresight; an instance of foolishness or rash behavior 愚笨（行为），蠢事

The ***folly*** of his youth caught up with him when he tried to get into college and his low high school grades and poor attendance record led to his rejection by all the schools he applied to. 由于年少贪玩，他高中成绩很糟，还经常缺课，所以申请大学入学时被所有他所申请的大学拒之门外。

▶ **imprudent**
/ɪmˈprudn̩t/
a.

unwise and indiscreet 不明智的；欠考虑的；轻率的

Mariah's ***imprudent*** behavior got her into trouble when her parents found out what she had been doing. 玛丽亚在父母发现她过去的所做所为后，因她欠妥的行为而使她陷入麻烦。

noun: **imprudence**
adverb: **imprudently**

▶ **inadvisable**
/ˌɪnədˈvaɪzəbl̩/

unwise and ill-considered, especially considering immediate circumstances 不明智的，不可取的

a.   Despite the action of many ice fishermen, it is ***inadvisable*** in northern states such as Minnesota and upper Michigan to drive a car onto a frozen lake after the first of March. 尽管许多冰上垂钓者会在三月上旬过后开车驶过冰冻的湖面，但在北方的明尼苏达州及密歇根上游地区，这样做是不可取的。

noun: **inadvisability**

▶ **inane**   lacking sense, substance, or logic 言之无物的，空洞的
/ɪn'en/

a.   Karl's comments were so often ***inane*** that no one listened to him anymore. 卡尔总是言之无物，因此没人再愿意听他讲话。

adverb: **inanely**

▶ **indiscreet**   lacking discretion or good judgment 不谨慎的，欠考虑的
/ˌɪndɪ'skrit/

a.   The politician's ***indiscreet*** behavior made him the target of Jay Leno's monologues long after he left office. 该政客的轻率举动使离任了很久的他成为杰伊·莱诺大肆取笑的对象。

noun: **indiscretion**
adverb: **indiscreetly**

▶ **inexpedient**   inadvisable; unwise, hindering 不妥当的，不明智的
/ˌɪnɪk'spidɪənt/

a.   The commander's orders were so ***inexpedient*** that even the lowest-ranking soldiers knew they were following a fool. 这个指挥官的命令都很欠妥当，即使是军衔最低的士兵都知道他们跟随的是个大傻瓜。

noun: **inexpediency**
adverb: **inexpediently**

►**injudicious** showing a lack of discretion or good judgment; unwise（行
/ˌɪndʒu'dɪʃəs/ 为或言论）判断不当的；不明智的
a.

> Henri's ***injudicious*** behavior, such as driving the wrong way
> down a one-way street, often got both of us in trouble, even
> though I was usually just along for the ride. 亨利的一些不
> 明智行为，比如在单行道上逆向开车，经常使我俩招惹
> 麻烦，尽管我通常只是坐车随行而已。

> adverb: **injudiciously**

►**ludicrous** foolish for laughable or hilarious reasons 荒唐可笑的
/'ludɪkrəs/
a.

> Nathan's solution to the problem was so ***ludicrous*** and
> improbable that we thought it just might work. 内森解决问
> 题的方法既可笑又无实施的可能，我们觉得行得通的几
> 率很小。

> noun: **ludicrousness**
> adverb: **ludicrously**

►**preposterous** contrary to common sense; foolish; not natural 反常的；荒
/prɪ'pɑstərəs/ 谬的；愚蠢的
a.

> Gloria's suggestion was ***preposterous***; we couldn't believe that
> anyone could come up with such a ridiculous idea. 格洛丽亚
> 的建议真是荒唐。我们都不相信竟然会有人提出这么可
> 笑的主意。

> adverb: **preposterously**

►**rash** hasty, poorly planned, and not well thought out; foolish
/ræʃ/ 急躁的，鲁莽的；愚蠢的
a.

> The coach's anger at his quarterback caused him to pull the
> player from the game, and many fans claimed that it was

this *rash* decision that caused the loss of the championship game. 教练出于对四分卫的不满而把他换下场，许多球迷认为这个草率的决定导致他们在冠军争夺赛中失利。

noun: **rashness**
adverb: **rashly**

▶ **witless**
/ˈwɪtlɪs/
a.

lacking intelligence, wit, or good sense 无才智的，愚蠢的

The bystander was a *witless* witness for the prosecution; he could not even recall if the accident took place during the day or at night. 诉讼中该目击证人的表现相当愚蠢，他甚至都不记得事件究竟是在白天还是夜晚发生的。

noun: **witlessness**
adverb: **witlessly**

Sentence Completion 完成句子

Circle the word or word pair that best completes the meaning of the sentence. 圈出最符合句子含义的词或一对词。

1. The U.S. purchase of Alaska was nicknamed Seward's
   _____, after Seward, who was responsible for what
   many considered a worthless purchase.
   A. inanity
   B. witlessness
   C. folly
   D. keenness
   E. sagacity

2. The _____ fox seemed to know exactly how to evade
   the hunters.
   A. canny
   B. judicious
   C. perceptive
   D. prudent
   E. shrewd

3. The new ruling was so _____ that few people could
   vote for such a _____ thing.
   A. preposterous/ludicrous
   B. injudicious/shrewd
   C. sapient/inane
   D. astute/judicious
   E. acute/keen

4. The experienced lawyer's mental _____ made him a fair and _____ judge.
   A. acuteness/rash
   B. witlessness/acute
   C. prudence/indiscreet
   D. politic/preposterous
   E. acumen/judicious

5. The circus clown's _____ antics demonstrated what a _____ he was.
   A. inadvisable/sage
   B. witless/buffoon
   C. rash/wit
   D. astute/prude
   E. shrewd/inanity

Quick Matching 快速配对

Write the letter of the definition shown in the right column next to the word that matches it in the left column. 在右栏中找出与左栏单词相符的定义，将对应的字母写在单词旁。

_____ 1. prudent	A. lacking good judgment
_____ 2. rash	B. unusually perceptive
_____ 3. keen	C. showing good judgment
_____ 4. injudicious	D. quick and mentally incisive
_____ 5. perspicacious	E. hasty and poorly planned

Complete the Story 完成故事

Using these words selected from this unit, fill in the blanks to complete the story. 用本单元的词汇填空，完成故事。

acumen	rash
shrewd	canny
sagacity	discernment
inane	sapient
astute	ludicrous
fatuous	folly
rash	perspicacious
injudicious	buffoon
keen	

_____ television marketers have realized that the _____ slapstick routines of early comedy teams such as Laurel and Hardy and the Three Stooges would not be successful with today's viewing audiences. Their _____ and _____ of public viewing tastes resulted in the long-running animated show known as *The Simpsons*.

The Simpsons are a curious family of five characters, four of whom are the center of much public amusement and sometimes private criticism. Homer Simpson, the father, is a _____ who means well, but whose _____ decisions and _____ behavior bring much humor to the program. In contrast to him is his wife Marge. Sometimes she is a _____ woman whose _____ mind acts as a good foil to husband Homer. However, she often finds herself in _____ situations with hilarious outcomes.

The baby of the family, who has not aged in the last dozen years, has no developed personality. However, the two older children, Bart and Lisa, make up for this. Bart is a mischievous boy whose _____ behavior and constant _____ keep the viewing audience entertained. Lisa is the smart, _____ member of this cartoon family. She demonstrates _____ and _____ understanding of almost every situation. She is a _____ observer of human nature, and, despite her youth, this wisdom offers a sharp, entertaining contrast to Bart's _____ actions.

ANSWERS 答案

Sentence Completion 完成句子：1-C, 2-B, 3-A, 4-E, 5-B

Quick Matching 快速配对：1-C, 2-E, 3-D, 4-A, 5-B

Complete the Story 完成故事：perspicacious, inane, acumen, discernment, buffoon, injudicious, fatuous, shrewd, canny, ludicrous, rash, folly, astute, sagacity, sapient, keen, rash

Roar Like a Lion or Mew Like a Kitten

狮子般怒吼还是猫咪般喵呜

有些人很安静很谦逊，就像春雨一般静静无声。你甚至会觉得在他们心中什么都不曾发生过。这些人平静、安详，一生波澜不惊。相比之下，还有些人总会让你意识到他们的存在；他们会让你联想到龙卷风。有时候，他们吵吵嚷嚷；更多时候他们让人操心；甚至让人恼火。然而，正是这两类人——以及两个极端之间的各种各样的人——共同让我们的生活丰富多彩。

appease	levelheaded	serene
assuage	mitigate	slack
composed	placate	sluggish
détente	placid	tranquility
dormant	quiescent	
imperturbable	repose	

....

blatant	din	ostentatious
boisterous	discordant	strident
brattle	fractious	truculent
brawl	hubbub	turbulent
clamorous	obstreperous	vociferous

► **appease**
/ə'piz/
v.

to pacify or make tranquil; to calm down or settle something or someone 平息，安抚

He claimed that the government had only changed the law in order to *appease* their critics. 他声称政府只是变更了法令来平息他们对政府的不满。

noun: **appeasement**

► **assuage**
/ə'swedʒ/
v.

to lessen; to take the edge off; to tone down 缓和，减轻

To *assuage* his hunger during the 50-mile bike trip, Marvin ate a granola bar. 为了减轻50英里自行车赛带来的饥饿感，马文吃下了一个格兰诺拉麦片棒。

noun: **assuagement**

► **composed**
/kəm'pozd/
a.

serene and self-possessed; calm and not easily agitated 镇定的，平静的

Maria was so *composed* that working in a day care center after school rarely fazed her. 玛丽亚做事淡定从容。即使放学后还要去托儿所工作，她也能做到有条不紊。

noun: **composure**
verb: **compose**

► **détente**
/de'tɑ̃t/
n.

a relaxing or easing of tensions between rivals, often, but not always, in a political sense（国际间紧张关系的）缓和

After the war in Iraq, it will take persistent and clever efforts to establish a *détente* between the United States and France. 伊拉克战争后，美法两国间关系的缓和将需要耐心和智慧。

► **dormant**
/'dɔrmənt/

lying asleep or in a calm state, but having the suggestion of life or activity that is temporarily quiet 休眠的，蛰伏的

a.

The grizzly bear was hungry after its ***dormant***, three-month sleep. 这只大灰熊在三个月的冬眠后变得很饥饿。

Sometimes cancer cells lie ***dormant*** for years before they become active. 有时候癌细胞在被激活之前，能数年保持休眠状态。

noun: **dormancy**
adverb: **dormantly**

▶**imperturbable** not easily shaken; calm, cool, and easygoing; slow to
/ˌɪmpɚ'tɜ·bəbl̩/ become excited 沉着的，不易激动的
a.

Marsha was ***imperturbable***; no matter what last-minute project her boss burdened her with, she remained unruffled. 玛莎行事沉着。无论老板施加给她多紧迫的任务，她都能从容面对。

adverb: **imperturbably**
noun: **imperturbability**

▶**levelheaded** usually composed and in control; not easily rattled or swayed
/ˌlɛvl̩'hɛdɪd/ by differing opinions 稳健的，头脑冷静的
a.

Because Jason is so ***levelheaded***, my mother thinks he will be a good influence on me. 母亲认为头脑冷静的贾森将给我做个好榜样。

noun: **levelheadedness**

▶**mitigate** to moderate in force or intensity; to calm or cool down; to
/'mɪtəˌget/ lessen in intensity 减轻，缓和
v.

Jerome was able to ***mitigate*** Tanya's anger by explaining the circumstances of his missing their date and promising to make it up to her the following weekend. 杰尔姆对错过约

会进行了解释，并承诺下周末弥补，使得塔尼娅的怒气缓和了许多。

noun: **mitigation**
adjective: **mitigated**

▶ **placate**
/'pleket/
v.

to appease, pacify, soothe, or make amends 安抚，使平静

The young mother was temporarily able to ***placate*** the fussy child by distracting him with a lollipop. 这位年轻的母亲用棒棒糖吸引了孩子的注意力，使焦躁不安的孩子暂时安静了下来。

noun: **placation**
adjective: **placatory**

▶ **placid**
/'plæsɪd/
a.

undisturbed, unflappable, calm, serene, and satisfied 平静的；平和的；满足的

There is nothing more relaxing than to sit by a ***placid*** lake on a warm summer day with nothing to think about other than when to return home for dinner. 暖暖夏日，坐在风平浪静的湖边，除了想想何时回家吃晚饭什么都不想——没有比这更惬意的事了！

adverb: **placidly**
noun: **placidity, placidness**

▶ **quiescent**
/kwaɪ'ɛsn̩t/
a.

quiet; still; at rest; serene and calm 静止的，不活动的，平静的

The ***quiescent*** child was deceptive, for her high energy and incessant demands were only temporarily at rest. 这个小孩现在很安静，但这只是假象，在进行短暂休息后，她会有使不完的力气，也会不停地提出各种要求。

noun: **quiescence**

adverb: **quiescently**

▶ **repose**
/rɪ'poz/
n., v.

noun: quiet tranquility; the state of being at rest or asleep 平静；休息，睡觉

My grandfather's *repose* was evident because we heard gentle snoring coming from his recliner, where he had dozed off. 祖父刚刚还在打瞌睡现在一定是睡着了，我们听到躺椅处传来了轻微的鼾声。

verb: to lie down or to lie at rest 躺下，休息

The patient *reposed* on the couch with his injured leg elevated. 病人躺在睡椅上休息，受伤的腿吊得高高的。

▶ **serene**
/sə'rin/
a.

quiet and unperturbed; unaffected by disturbance; at peace within oneself 宁静的，安详的

Alice was so *serene* that, at the championship football game, the noise and enthusiasm around her barely made an impression on her. 艾丽斯总是不为外界所扰。足球冠军争夺赛上，周围喧闹声、加油声都很难影响到她。

adverb: **serenely**

noun: **serenity**

▶ **slack**
/slæk/
a.

slow moving, even lacking in activity; sluggish and unproductive 呆滞的；萧条的

In the automobile industry, the weeks before the changeover to next year's models tend to be a *slack* time at the manufacturing plants, thereby allowing maintenance crews the opportunity to service the machinery. 汽车行业在转组生产下一年模型之前的几个星期里，其制造部门会有一段停滞期，以使维修人员有机会对设备进行维修。

adverb: **slackly**

▶ **sluggish** displaying little growth or movement; not making progress;
/ˈslʌgɪʃ/ seeming to be bottlenecked or clogged to prevent advancement
a. 行动缓慢的，反映迟缓的

Traffic on the highway was *sluggish*, so many drivers took
nearby exits, trying to avoid the bottleneck. 道路上车行缓
慢，许多司机从邻近的出口驶出，以避开拥堵处。

adverb: **sluggishly**
noun: **slug**

▶ **tranquility** harmony; silence; quiet serenity; undisturbed and peaceful
/træŋˈkwɪlətɪ/ 和谐；平静；安谧
n.

Because Marta found such *tranquility* at the lake, she often
went there to unwind when she was upset or stressed about
her parents or schoolwork. 玛尔塔感受到湖边的静谧。只
要心情不好或是受父母的指责及学业压得喘不过气时，
她就会到湖边散心。

adjective: **tranquil**
adverb: **tranquilly**

• •

▶ **blatant** unpleasantly loud; irritatingly showy or obvious 公然的，
/ˈbletn̩t/ 贸然的
a.

The students displayed *blatant* disrespect for the principal
when, after he had just spoken to them about proper
behavior in the auditorium, they continued to whisper and
carry on with no courtesy for the guest speaker. 校长刚刚跟
学生讲了在礼堂的行为举止，学生们竟公然藐视校长，
继续交头接耳对特邀演讲人毫不尊敬。

adverb: **blatantly**

noun: **blantancy**

▶ **boisterous**
/ˈbɔɪstərəs/
a.

rowdy, rambunctious, and possibly out of control 喧闹的，活泼的

The kindergarteners, who had consumed too much sugar at the birthday party, were *boisterous*. 这些幼儿园的孩子在生日宴会上吃了太多的糖果，一个个活蹦乱跳的。

adverb: **boisterously**

▶ **brattle**
/ˈbrætl̩/
n.

a rattling and crashing sound 撞击声

The *brattle* of his armor made it impossible for the knight to sneak up on his enemy. 走动时铠甲发出的响声使这个骑士很难跟踪敌人。

▶ **brawl**
/brɔl/
v.,n.,a

verb: to have a loud and boisterous disagreement, possibly even a fight, but more likely just upsetting the calm and quiet 争吵，打架

Stefan was suspended when he *brawled* on the playground three times in one week. 斯蒂芬因一周三次在游乐场闹事而被停职。

noun: a loud, boisterous disagreement 争吵

During the Superbowl, a *brawl* erupted at a local sports bar. 美国橄榄球超级联赛期间，当地一家运动酒吧里发生了吵架斗殴事件。

adjective: brawling or brawly 喧闹的

By the end of three overtimes, the drunken, *brawling* crowd around the bar was disturbing everyone in the restaurant. 三

番拖延时间后，酒吧旁醉醺醺吵吵闹闹的一群人对餐馆里的其他人造成了很大干扰。

▶ **clamorous**
/'klæmə·rəs/
a.

characterized by a loud, even discordant, noise, outcry, or insistent, disturbing racket 吵闹的，喧嚷的

The sound of the *clamorous* fire alarm in the middle of the night was disruptive to everyone in the dorm. 半夜火灾的警报声惊扰了寝室里的每个人。

noun: **clamor**
adverb: **clamorously**

▶ **din**
/dɪn/
n.

disorder and noise; tumult and confusion 喧闹声，嘈杂声

The *din* in the cafeteria during lunch period was so great that my friends and I couldn't have a conversation without our having to yell at one another. 午餐时间自助餐厅里人声鼎沸，我和朋友们不得不扯着嗓门说话。

▶ **discordant**
/dɪs'kɔrdn̩t/
a.

clashing in ideas or sound or philosophies; harsh with conflict 不一致的，不和谐的，相互冲突的

The *discordant* notes he played on the piano were unsettling to me, and the hair on the cat stood up and he began to hiss. 他在钢琴上奏出的不和谐音使我心神不宁，就连猫的毛都竖起来了，开始嘶嘶地叫。

noun: **discord**
adverb: **discordantly**

▶ **fractious**
/'frækʃəs/
a.

• unruly and noisy 不安分的，烦躁的

The *fractious* pre-schoolers were out of control. 不安分的学龄前孩子都不好管教。

- cranky or peevish 易怒的，乖张的

The *fractious* child had missed her nap and was trying everyone's patience with her whining and snuffling. 这个性格乖张的孩子错过了午睡，正在用哀诉和抽泣挑战人们的忍耐极限。

noun: **fractiousness**
adverb: **fractiously**

▶ **hubbub**
/'hʌbʌb/
n.

an upset or vehement protest or discontent; sometimes a loud, sustained noise 喧闹声，嘈杂声

The unexpected victory of the underdog soccer team created such a *hubbub* that the police were called in to quell the disturbances and prevent a riot. 球队出人意料的反败为胜引发了骚乱，警方不得不出动以防止混乱场面越演愈烈。

▶ **obstreperous**
/əb'strɛpərəs/
a.

noisy and boisterous; sometimes even aggressive or defiant 喧哗的，吵嚷的，任性的

The toddler's behavior became *obstreperous* when he refused to lie down for a nap. 这个初学走路的孩子拒绝躺下来午睡，开始大吵大闹。

adverb: **obstreperously**
noun: **obstreperousness**

▶ **ostentatious**
/ˌɑstən'teʃəs/
a.

showy; characterized by a need to be noticed, not always favorably 卖弄的，炫耀的

The house was an *ostentatious* disaster of architecture — every possible ornament had been added to the design without regard to appropriateness or style. 这座房子在设计上甚为卖弄，是建筑上的败笔——集各式装饰于一身，

全然不顾风格的统一和谐。

adverb: **ostentatiously**
noun: **ostentation**

▶**strident**
/'straɪdṇt/
a.

loud and harsh; often grating and discordant; hard on the ears 尖声的，刺耳的

The *strident* tornado siren alerted everyone to the impending danger, and people went to their basements or safe rooms if they had them. 刺耳的龙卷风警报使人们感到了危险的迫近，有条件的人都躲进了地下室或安全的房间。

adverb: **stridently**
noun: **stridency**

▶**truculent**
/'trʌkjələnt/
a.

tending to argue and disagree, often vehemently and with great noise and commotion 脾气暴躁的

The homeless man, who was usually quite easygoing, became *truculent* when someone tried to take over his comfortable spot under the bridge. 当有人试图霸占他桥底下舒适的小窝时，这个平时很随和的流浪汉变得很暴躁。

noun: **truculence**
adverb: **truculently**

▶**turbulent**
/'tɜːbjələnt/
a.

• violently upset or disturbed 狂暴的

After the torrential rains, the water in the nearby creek was *turbulent* and swiftly swept away great tree limbs and other debris. 暴雨使得附近的河水泛滥，并很快冲走了大树枝和其他碎片。

• having a restless or even revolutionary character 动乱的，骚动的

The political climate was so *turbulent* that the local tribal leader did not dare to leave the village for fear that someone else would be in control of it upon his return. 政局动荡使得当地族长不敢离开村庄，以免他人趁机控制村庄。

noun: **turbulence**
adverb: **turbulently**

► **vociferous**
/vo'sɪfərəs/
a.

offensively loud and often given to demonstration of agitated emotions or agitated outcry（发牢骚、表示不满时）吵吵嚷嚷的

Local activist groups have become increasingly *vociferous* as the volume of traffic passing through the village has grown. 当经过这个村庄的车流量增长时，地方激进主义者团体变得日益情绪激昂，吵吵嚷嚷表示不满。

noun: **vociferousness**
adverb: **vociferously**

Sentence Completion 完成句子

Circle the word or word pair that best completes the meaning of the sentence. 圈出最符合句子含义的词或一对词。

1. After lying _____ during the cold winter, the tulip and daffodil bulbs began to sprout beneath the warming soil.
   A. repose
   B. détente
   C. sluggishly
   D. dormant
   E. serenely

2. Normally quiet and _____, Jerome amazed everyone when he got into a noisy _____ at the Pizza Palace when some of his so-called friends started to taunt him after the football game.
   A. imperturbable/brawl
   B. fractious/din
   C. levelheaded/truculence
   D. quiescent/discord
   E. ostentation/hubbub

3. The high-strung young bronco became _____ during the rodeo; even the most experienced handlers were unable to bring him under control.
   A. turbulent
   B. truculent
   C. boisterous
   D. vociferous
   E. ostentatious

4. After the torrential spring rains, the slow and often _____
   creek became dangerously _____.
   A. slack/strident
   B. sluggish/turbulent
   C. serene/brawling
   D. composed/discordant
   E. placid/blatant

5. The ear-splitting _____ of the alarm created such a
   _____ that no one could hear the fire marshal as he
   gave orders to the firefighters.
   A. hubbub/brattle
   B. turbulence/discord
   C. clamor/din
   D. brawl/vociferousness
   E. stridency/détente

Quick Matching 快速配对

*Write the letter of the definition shown in the right column next
to the word that matches it in the left column.* 在右栏中找出与
左栏单词相符的定义，将对应的字母写在单词旁。

_____1. assuage

_____2. mitigate

_____3. placate

_____4. repose

_____5. brawl

A. to moderate the force or
   intensity

B. to lie down to rest

C. to disagree in a loud and
   boisterous manner

D. to lessen or tone down

E. to appease, pacify, soothe, or
   make amends

Complete the Story 完成故事

Using these words selected from this unit, fill in the blanks to complete the story. 用本单元的词汇填空，完成故事。

quiescent	truculent
boisterous	levelheaded
imperturbable	discord
placate	détente
din	placatory
serene	fractious
vociferously	placid
clamorous	composed

My Uncle Rondo recently served on a jury. The case was a complicated one, and there was so much conflicting evidence that the jury had a difficult time reaching a verdict. It was the makeup of the group, however, that made things especially difficult.

Uncle Rondo said that the first job the jurors had was to elect a foreperson for the group. This had to be a _____ person who would lead the group and not get carried away by emotional arguments. They decided on a retired air-traffic controller, who was calm and _____, not surprising when you consider that his career had demanded that he remain _____ under stressful conditions. Two young, quiet, office workers were also on the jury. One was laid back and _____, and the other had a _____ nature. Since Uncle Rondo is _____ himself and always likes everyone to get along, he liked these two right away.

In contrast to this calm, _____ group were four rather

_____ jury members who often had to be reminded to get back to the business of the moment. In fact, Uncle Rondo said they got so loud and _____ one day that the bailiff had to come in to the room where they were working and quiet the _____. After that, these three settled down to the job at hand.

Unfortunately, however, there were also four _____ hotheads in the group. They were quick to disagree, and they would argue _____. A couple of times the foreperson had to _____ hurt feelings because of the _____ behavior of these people. Until these four settled down, it was hard for the jury to get anywhere. Eventually a _____ was reached; everybody resolved to avoid further _____, and the jury was able to complete its task.

Uncle Rondo said that he learned a lot about the law by being on a jury during the two weeks of the trial and the two weeks it took them to reach a verdict. However, what he found the most interesting was what happens when twelve strangers, with very different personalities, have to work together toward a common goal.

ANSWERS 答案

Sentence Completion 完成句子： 1-D, 2-A, 3-B, 4-B, 5-C

Quick Matching 快速配对： 1-D, 2-A, 3-E, 4-B, 5-C

Complete the Story 完成故事： levelheaded, imperturbable, composed, serene, quiescent, placatory, placid, boisterous, clamorous, din, truculent, vociferously, placate, fractious, détente, discord

Something Old, Something New
一些陈旧，一些新颖

年轻人一般都不愿意让别人认为自己很年轻，而有些老年人也不喜欢被别人认为自己已经老了。幸运的是，我们的语言为我们提供了许多词汇来满足我们的要求。有些相对来说容易接受；有些则不那么被人们接受。无论如何，下列这些词汇可以为你提供丰富的选择，来描述关于年轻和年老的概念。

budding	innovation	proselyte
burgeoning	naive	raw
embryonic	nascent	rudimentary
fledgling	neophyte	shaver
incipient	neoteric	stripling
initiate	postulant	untried

antediluvian	gerontic	primitive
antiquated	hoary	primordial
archaic	obsolescence	seasoned
dateless	outmoded	superannuated
fossilized	passé	venerable
full-fledged	prehistoric	veteran
geriatric	primeval	

► **budding**
/'bʌdɪŋ/
a.

having to do with new or developing circumstances or abilities 开始发育的，初露头角的

The ***budding*** artist was excited about his first gallery show. 这位初露头角的艺术家为自己的第一场画展兴奋不已。

► **burgeoning**
/'bɝdʒənɪŋ/
a.

growing or developing; blossoming or flourishing 迅速发展的

The ***burgeoning*** business had a rocky beginning, but soon it became a solid company worth millions of dollars. 这家发展得很好的公司刚开始很艰难，但不久就成长为一家价值几百万美元实力雄厚的公司了。

verb: **burgeon**

► **embryonic**
/ˌɛmbrɪ'ɑnɪk/
a.

of or belonging to an embryo; early beginning; not yet formed or matured; rudimentary 胚胎期的，萌芽期的

The bird was in its ***embryonic*** stage when the egg fell out of the nest onto the patio. 当蛋从鸟窝里掉到院子里时，这只鸟还处在胚胎期。

noun: **embryo**

► **fledgling**
/'flɛdʒlɪŋ/
a.

new or immature; not yet out of the nest; not experienced; rudimentary 初出茅庐的

The ***fledgling*** foreign reporter was anxious to get his story so he did not take his own safety into consideration during the mission. 这位初出茅庐的外国记者在履行这次任务时急切地想采访到新闻，因而没有考虑到自己的安全。

► **incipient**
/ɪn'sɪpɪənt/
a.

beginning to exist or appear; early in developmental stage 刚出现的；早期的

The architect's plans were still in their ***incipient*** stage when the builder broke ground for the new structure. 当工人们开始挖地修建新建筑时，建筑师的规划才刚刚开始。

adverb: **incipiently**
noun: **incipience**

▶ **initiate**
/ɪ'nɪʃɪˌet/
n., v.

noun: one who is being or has been initiated; one who has been introduced to or has attained knowledge in a particular field 入门者；被传授了专门知识的人

verb: to begin or start a process; to get things going 创始，发起；开始实施

The *initiate* met the visitors at the door, ready to *initiate* them into the world of art. 这位专家在门口接见了访问者，并准备将他们带入艺术的世界。

adverb: **initially**
noun (variation): **initiation**

▶ **innovation**
/ɪnə'veʃən/
n.

the act of introducing something or someone; something newly introduced 创新；新发明

Myra's *innovation* was so creative that everyone was enthusiastic about following it up. 迈拉的新方法很富有创造性，人人都热衷于效仿。

verb: **innovate**
adjective: **innovative**

▶ **naive**
/nɑ'iv/
a.

untried and inexperienced; not knowledgeable or practiced 幼稚的，无经验的

The *naive* youngsters were easily led astray by the older students, while the teachers seemed oblivious to what was going on. 这些幼稚的年轻人很容易就受到年长学

生的影响而误入歧途，而老师们却似乎对此并无察觉。

noun: **naïveté, naiveness**
adverb: **naively**

▶ **nascent**
/'næsn̩t/

coming into existence, emerging 初生的；新出现的

a.

The committee had several *nascent* ideas for the new project, but nothing was decided by the end of the meeting. 委员会对这个新项目有一些新想法，但到会议结束时也没有做出任何决定。

noun: **nascence**
adverb: **nascently**

▶ **neophyte**
/'niə,faɪt/

a recent convert; a novice or beginner 新入教者；初学者，新手

n.

The youngster was a mere *neophyte*; he had no experience but only a mind full of dreams. 这个年轻人只是个初学者，没有经验，满脑子只有幻想。

▶ **neoteric**
/,nio'tɛrɪk/

of recent emergence; beginning; modern 新发明的，新的

a.

The ideas were *neoteric*, and because they had never been tried or tested, many of them were useless. 这些想法都是新的，由于从未经实践检验过，因此许多都没有用。

▶ **postulant**
/'pɑstʃələnt/

new to a situation; a petitioner or someone who is starting out on a new endeavor 神职申请人，准备担任圣职的人

a.

The *postulant* nun had just joined the convent, and she found that following all the rules was more difficult than she had ever imagined. 这位申请神职的修女刚加入了女修道院，她发现遵守所有的规定比原来想象的要难。

► **proselyte**
/ˈprɑslˌaɪt/
n.

a newcomer or someone newly converted; novice or beginner
改变宗教或政治信仰者；新手

The Brownie scout was a true *proselyte* of the Girl Scouts —
she couldn't wait to put on her uniform and start selling
cookies. 这个女童子军真是一个新手。她迫不及待地要
穿上制服，开始贩卖曲奇饼。

verb: **proselytize**

► **raw**
/rɔ/
a.

uncooked or untried; inexperienced; unpracticed; experimental
生的，未煮过的；未经训练的，没有经验的

The new Marine recruits were so *raw* that their buzz haircuts
sat uncomfortably on their heads. 这些新入伍的海军士
兵未经任何训练，一个个都是刚刚理过的板寸头，很
不自然。

noun: **rawness**
adverb: **rawly**

► **rudimentary**
/ˌrudəˈmɛntərɪ/
a.

elementary; being in the earliest stages of development
基本的，基础的，初步的

The students' knowledge of math was *rudimentary* since
they could barely do more than add and subtract. 学生们的
数学知识很粗浅，因为他们只会加减法。

noun: **rudiment**

► **shaver**
/ˈʃevɚ/
n.

informal, somewhat colloquial expression used to describe
a young boy; one without experience 男孩子

Many critics view Huckleberry Finn as a young *shaver*, out
of his league in his journey down the Mississippi River;
other critics recognize Huck as the mouthpiece of Mark

Twain himself. 许多评论家认为，哈克贝利·费恩相对于游历密西西比河的其他同伴来说是个没有经验的年轻人，而另一些评论家则认为哈克就是马克·吐温的代言人。

▶ **stripling**
/ˈstrɪplɪŋ/
n.

an adolescent male 小伙子

Every action of the seasoned hunters was closely observed by Georgio's nephew, a *stripling* who accompanied the men on their hunting trip. 乔治的侄子是一个陪伴这些经验丰富的猎人们打猎的年轻人，他密切注视着这些猎人的一举一动。

▶ **untried**
/ʌnˈtraɪd/
a.

not tried or experienced; fledgling; without skill or knowledge 未试过的，没有经验的

The young retriever was *untried*, but she did a good job of retrieving on her first duck hunt. 小猎狗没有经验，却在第一次的猎鸭行动中干得很好。

....

▶ **antediluvian**
/ˌæntɪdɪˈluvɪən/
a.

extremely old; usually, historically a reference to the era before the Flood 古老的

The forest was *antediluvian*; some of the trees had been alive since the prehistoric times. 这是个原始森林，有些树在史前时期就已存在。

▶ **antiquated**
/ˈæntəˌkwetɪd/
a.

too old to be fashionable or contemporary in thinking or style; very old or aged 过时的，陈旧的，老式的

The *antiquated* clothing of the Not New Shop attracted many partygoers on Halloween. "不新商店"的老式服装在万圣节那天吸引了许多社交聚会的常客。

verb: **antiquate**
noun: **antiquatedness**

▶**archaic**
/ɑrˈkeɪɪk/
a.

out of date; old; out of style, fashion, or contemporary thinking 过时的，陈旧的

The equipment in the medical clinic was *archaic*; all of it had been purchased before 1970. 诊所里的设备过时了，都是在1970年以前购买的。

adverb: **archaically**
noun: **archaism**

▶**dateless**
/ˈdetlɪs/
a.

having no date; so ancient that no date can be determined; having no limits in time; timeless 年代不详的；无期限的

The woman's dress was expensive, classic, and *dateless*; she might have worn it 30 years ago, or she might have purchased it in the last few months. 这个女人的裙子十分昂贵，样式经典，而且看不出任何的时代特征；她也许30年前就已经穿着了，也有可能是近几个月才买的。

▶**fossilize**
/ˈfɑslˌaɪz/
v.

convert to a fossil; make outmoded or inflexible with time 石化

The syrup had been in the pantry for so long that it had *fossilized* into a solid mass inside the bottle. 糖浆在食品室里存放太久了，已经在瓶中化为一种固态物质了。

noun: **fossil**

▶**full-fledged**
/ˌfʊlˈflɛdʒd/
a.

fully developed or mature; attaining full rank, status, or experience 发展成熟的；经过充分训练的

The cadets had gone through months of boot camp until finally, upon graduation, they became *full-fledged* soldiers. 这些军官学校的学生在新兵训练营里受训了几个月，到毕业时，他们最终成为了合格的士兵。

▶ **geriatric**
/ˌdʒɛrɪ'ætrɪk/
a.

of or related to the aged or the aging process 老年医学的

The medical intern concentrated her studies in *geriatric* research. 这个医学实习生主要研究老年医学。

noun: **geriatrics**
adverb: **geriatrically**

▶ **gerontic**
/dʒə'rɑntɪk/
a.

of or relating to very old age; having to do with the last stage of life 年迈的；临终的

All the men playing chess, though *gerontic*, were quick and clever strategists. 所有下象棋的人尽管已经年迈，但都机敏、聪颖，很有谋略。

noun: **gerontocracy, gerontology**

▶ **hoary**
/'hɔrɪ/
a.

white or gray, as with age 人因上了年纪而毛发花白的

The old beggar nodded his *hoary* head when I put money into his outstretched hand. 当我把钱放到头发花白的老乞丐伸出的手上时，他朝我点了点头。

▶ **obsolescence**
/ˌɑbsə'lɛsəns/
n.

something out of use or need; a dying breed or of unnecessary or unimportant need 荒废，退化，过时

The car's *obsolescence* was obvious because it could not run on lead-free gasoline. 这辆车很明显要报废了，因为它不能靠无铅汽油发动了。

adjective: **obsolescent, obsolete**

▶ **outmoded**
/ˌaʊt'modɪd/
a.

out of fashion; of no more use, need, or practicality 过时的；废弃的

Last year's styles may be *outmoded*, but Tanisha could not

afford to replace her wardrobe. 去年的服装样式可能已经过时了，但是塔妮莎没钱买新衣服。

▶ **passé**
/pæ'se/
a.

out of mode or fashion 过时的，老式的

Although it is *passé* for a man to tip his hat to a woman, many people still consider it a gentlemanly gesture. 尽管男士为女士以手触帽致敬的礼仪已经过时，但人们依旧认为这个举止很有绅士风度。

▶ **prehistoric**
/ˌprihɪs'tɔrɪk/
a.

of or relating to prehistory; slang — old and out of touch 史前的；（俚）老式的，老掉牙的

Archeology is the study of *prehistoric* civilizations. 考古学研究史前文明。

adverb: **prehistorically**
noun: **prehistory**

▶ **primeval**
/praɪ'mivl̩/
a.

from the earliest times or ages; original or ancient 古老的；原始的

The *primeval* swamps of the Florida Everglades are the setting for many horror and monster movies. 佛罗里达湿地的原始沼泽是许多恐怖电影和怪物电影的取景地。

▶ **primitive**
/'prɪmətɪv/
a.

primary or basic; of or relating to an earliest or original stage or state; primeval 基础的；原始的，初期的

My aunt still owns a *primitive* black-and-white television set. 我婶婶仍然拥有一台老旧的黑白电视机。

noun: **primitiveness**
adverb: **primitively**

▶ **primordial**

early in the developmental stage; basic and ancient 初生

/praɪˈmɔrdɪəl/（发）的；原始的，古老的
a.

Many American horror movies rely on touching the *primordial* fear within the audience — that same feeling we have when things go bump in the night. 许多美国恐怖电影都依赖于触动观众原始的恐惧感——就是在夜里遇到发出怪声的鬼怪时我们都会产生的感觉。

adverb: **primordially**

▶ **seasoned**
/ˈsiznd/
a.

characterized by experience, skill, or practice 很有经验的，训练有素的

The football player had been in the game for 15 years and was a *seasoned* veteran of the gridiron. 这名橄榄球运动员已经踢了15年了，是球场上有经验的老手。

▶ **superannuated**
/ˌsupɚˈænjuˌetɪd/
a.

retired or outmoded; no longer in use or needed 退休的；过时的；废旧的

The librarians took inventory of the shelves and discarded all the *superannuated* books and magazines. 图书管理员们清理了书架，把所有废旧的书籍和杂志都扔了。

▶ **venerable**
/ˈvɛnərəbl/
a.

worthy of respect or reverence; honorable 德高望众的，令人崇敬的

Many cultures consider their ancestors as *venerable* fonts of wisdom. 许多文明都将其祖先视为令人尊敬的智慧的化身。

noun: **venerability, venerableness**
adverb: **venerably**

▶ **veteran**
/ˈvɛtərən/

a person who is long experienced or practiced in an activity or capacity; often associated with past military personnel 经验

n.   丰富的人（尤指退伍军人）

The aged *veterans* marched proudly in their old uniforms on the eleventh of November. 年迈的退伍军人们在11月11日这天穿着旧军装自豪地行进着。

Sentence Completion 完成句子

Circle the word or word pair that best completes the meaning of the sentence. 圈出最符合句子含义的词或一对词。

1. The _____ company got off to a rocky start, but soon business picked up and it was firmly grounded.
   A. incipient
   B. fledgling
   C. stripling
   D. dateless
   E. primitive

2. The _____ computer was not worth salvaging; it should have been replaced several years ago.
   A. primeval
   B. veteran
   C. obsolescent
   D. burgeoning
   E. incipient

3. My niece is a _____ ballerina; she has barely conquered the most _____ of moves.
   A. shaver/archaic
   B. budding/rudimentary
   C. primitive/superannuated
   D. neoteric/untried
   E. primeval/passé

4. The Egyptian mummy was _____; since it predated most of recorded history, it quickly became a(n) _____ example of antiquity.

A. prehistoric/full-fledged

B. hoary/primeval

C. embryonic/incipient

D. geriatric/hoary

E. outmoded/seasoned

5. The police officer was hardly a(n) _____; he had been with the force for over 25 years, and many referred to him as the _____.

A. fledgling/neophyte

B. initiate/proselyte

C. shaver/fossil

D. gerontic/geriatric

E. obsolescence/innovation

Quick Matching 快速配对

Write the letter of the definition shown in the right column next to the word that matches it in the left column. 在右栏中找出与左栏单词相符的定义，将对应的字母写在单词旁。

_____1. primeval   A. early developmental stage

_____2. dateless   B. late developmental stage

_____3. gerontic   C. ancient and original in origin

_____4. nascent   D. having no limits in time; timeless

_____5. incipient   E. emerging; coming into existence

Complete the Story 完成故事

Using these words selected from this unit, fill in the blanks to complete the story. 用本单元的词汇填空，完成故事。

full-fledged	superannuated
rudimentary	geriatric
primeval	dateless
neophyte	antiquated
outmoded	budding
fossilized	postulant
embryonic	primitive
stripling	

Great Britain—England, Wales, Ireland, and Scotland—is a land of many contrasts. A visitor to this land can walk through _____ forests or a _____ metropolis on the same day. Great Britain's history is almost _____. It boasts many fine examples of _____ civilizations. In fact, many _____ remains have been unearthed in peat bogs, and an archeological dig, known as Sutton Hoo, revealed the remnants of a _____ Anglo-Saxon ship and all its contents buried beneath the fields of a modest farmer. Treasures from this archeological dig included _____ weapons and _____ jewelry.

Cities such as London, Dublin, and Glasgow also provide many contrasts. _____, _____ travelers are usually amazed at these cities. They will find many conveniences along with _____ plumbing and air conditioning. Although Americans often find British amenities _____, there is no doubt that the nation is far from _____. In fact, Great Britain seems _____ in contrast to the _____ "colonies."

ANSWERS 答案

Sentence Completion 完成句子：1-B, 2-C, 3-B, 4-A, 5-C

Quick Matching 快速配对：1-C, 2-D, 3-B, 4-E, 5-A

Complete the Story 完成故事：primeval, budding, dateless, primitive, fossilized, full-fledged, antiquated, rudimentary, Neophyte, postulant, superannuated, outmoded, embryonic, geriatric, stripling

Review 2 复习 2

These sentences include words from the previous four units. 下列句子需要使用前面四个单元的词汇。

Sentence Completion 完成句子

Circle the word pair that best completes the meaning of the sentence. 圈出最符合句子含义的一对词。

1. The _____ giant swamp lizard exuded a _____ odor as it came close to the hunters.
   A. alluring/perceptive
   B. obstreperous/nascent
   C. uncouth/sluggish
   D. primordial/feral
   E. shrewd/radiant

2. Although it was _____ to think that she could keep up with the other experienced riders, Marta was _____ in her determination not to fall behind, so she kept on pedaling, despite aching muscles.
   A. ludicrous/obstreperous
   B. prudent/discordant
   C. innovative/churlish
   D. inadvisable/levelheaded
   E. shrewd/novel

3. The young T-ball players were _____ when it came to the strategies of baseball, so they seldom demonstrated much _____ as to where to throw the ball.
A. barbarians/folly
B. resplendent/astuteness
C. neophytes/acumen
D. boisterous/indiscretion
E. quiescent/sagacity

4. The factory was old, and much of the equipment was _____; nevertheless, the new owner was _____ enough to see the potential of the location of the building and the good reputation of the company name.
A. ostentatious/vulgar
B. outmoded/vociferous
C. untried/politic
D. archaic/perceptive
E. burgeoning/serene

5. Although the young woman was usually dressed in a rather _____ manner, she demonstrated such _____ in her job as a lawyer's assistant that he started turning to her for advice.
A. coarse/indiscretion
B. salacious/perspicacity
C. placid/serenity
D. rash/boisterousness
E. obsolete/tranquility

ANSWERS 答案

1-D, 2-A, 3-C, 4-D, 5-B

SECTION III

Unit 1 **Friend or Foe** 朋友还是敌人 ►accommodating, affable, amiable, amicable, compatible, complaisant, concurrent, congruent, convivial, cordial, genial, harmonious, like-minded, obliging ►aloof, arrogant, contemptuous, derisive, disdainful, egocentric, haughty, incongruous, pompous, priggish, reticent, sanctimonious, self-aggrandizing, self-righteous, self-satisfied, smug, supercilious

Unit 2 **Give or Receive** 给予还是接受 ►abstemious, chintzy, closefisted, frugal, meager, mercenary, miserly, niggardly, parsimonious, penurious, provident, stingy ►altruistic, benevolent, bounteous, eleemosynary, lavish, magnanimous, munificent, openhandedly, philanthropy, selfless, self-sacrificing, unstinting

Unit 3 **Commend or Condemn** 称赞还是谴责 ►acclaim, admirable, applaud, approbation, celebrate, citation, creditable, encomium, esteem, eulogy, extol, kudo, laudable, meritorious, panegyric, praiseworthy ►abominate, admonitory, berate, blameworthy, castigate, censurable, culpable, decry, denounce, deplore, deprecate, despise, disparage, excoriate, objurgate, reprehensible, reproachful, reprove

Unit 4 **Fortitude and Foolhardiness** 刚毅还是蛮勇►audacious, bravado, dauntless, defiance, fortitude, gallant, intrepid, plucky, resolute, stalwart, steadfast, tenacious, valiant, virago ►brash, capricious, daring, derring-do, foolhardy, hotheaded, impetuous, impulsive, insolent, madcap, offhanded, perilous, rash, reckless, temerity

Unit 5 **One Size Does *Not* Fit All** 一种规格不可能处处合适 ►dearth, diminutive, infinitesimal, insignificant, Lilliputian, meager, minuscule, minute, mite, negligible, paucity, petty, pittance, scant, scintilla, trifling, trivial ►ample, behemoth, Brobdingnagian, colossal, copious, gargantuan, humongous, immeasurable, incalculable, infinite, mammoth, monumental, plethora, prodigious, statuesque, surfeit, titanic

Friend or Foe
朋友还是敌人

我们如何选择朋友？一般来说我们都努力躲开那些*傲慢的* (*arrogant*)、眼里只有自己的人。*自鸣得意的* (*smug*)、*居高自傲的* (*disdainful*) 人反正也不会来搭理我们。而我们最不愿意做的就是与*虚伪的* (*sanctimonious*)、*自以为是的* (*self-righteous*) 或者目空一切的 (*supercilious*) 人待在一起。没有人会欣赏那种唯我独尊的态度。

我们喜欢的是与*亲切的* (*amiable*)、*志趣相投的* (*compatible*) 人交朋友。熟人一般来说都是*友好的* (*convivial*)、*亲切的* (*genial*) 人，他们的个性与我们的性格十分*和谐* (*harmonious*)。幸运的是，我们的语言赋予我们大量词汇来描述我们愿意共处的人和极力避开的人。

accommodating	complaisent	genial
affable	concurrent	harmonious
amiable	congruent	like-minded
amicable	convivial	obliging
compatible	cordial	

....

aloof	haughty	self-aggrandizing
arrogant	incongruous	self-righteous
contemptuous	pompous	self-satisfied
derisive	priggish	smug
disdainful	reticent	supercilious

► **accommodating** helpful and obliging 乐于助人的
/əˈkɑməˌdetɪŋ/

a. The police officer was ***accommodating*** as he helped us figure out where we were going. 这个警官热心助人，他帮助我们弄清楚了我们正往哪走。

adverb: **accommodatingly**
noun: **accommodation**
verb: **accommodate**

► **affable** easy and pleasant to speak to; approachable and gracious 容易交谈的；友善的
/ˈæfəbl̩/

a. Possibly thinking ahead to her tip, the waitress gave us an ***affable*** smile as she took our order. 女服务员也许想要小费，在服务时对我们友善地一笑。

adverb: **affably**
noun: **affability**

► **amiable** friendly and agreeable in disposition; good-natured, likable, and sociable 友善的；和蔼可亲的
/ˈemɪəbl̩/

a. Because Yer was an ***amiable*** woman, she rarely met a person who didn't become her friend. 因为叶是一个友善的女人，所以她遇到的人通常都会成为她的朋友。

adverb: **amiably**
noun: **amiability**

► **amicable** characterized by or showing friendliness 友好的
/ˈæmɪkəbl̩/

a. Lauren was so ***amicable*** that everyone seemed to like her. 劳伦十分友好，每个人似乎都很喜欢她。

noun: **amicability**
adverb: **amicably**

► **compatible**
/kəmˈpætəbl̩/
a.

existing or performing in harmonious, agreeable, or congenial combination with another or others 可以并存的，相容的，协调的

Amy and Ray are a *compatible* couple; not only are they husband and wife, but they are best friends as well. 埃米和雷是很合得来的一对，他们不仅是夫妻，还是最好的朋友。

adverb: **compatibly**
noun: **compatibility**

► **complaisant**
/kəmˈpleznt̩/
a.

exhibiting a desire or willingness to please; cheerfully obliging 殷勤的，讨好的；谦恭的

Because golden retrievers have a very strong need to please their masters, they are considered *complaisant* house pets. 金毛猎犬有强烈的愿望去讨好主人，因此它们被认为是讨人喜欢的宠物。

adverb: **complaisantly**
noun: **complaisance**

► **concurrent**
/kənˈkɜ·ənt/,
concurring
/kənˈkɜ·rɪŋ/
a.

in accordance with other things or persons; harmonious; in agreement 并存的，同时发生的；和谐的；一致的

Because the time of the history class was *concurrent* with the time of the English class, I had to make a choice. 因为历史课和英语课在同一时间，所以我得做一个选择。

The mother was glad to see her usually squabbling boys were *concurring* with one another. 妈妈见到总是相互争吵的儿子们此时相处融洽很是高兴。

noun: **concurrence**
verb: **concur**

▶ **congruent**
/'kɑŋgruənt/
a.

being in sync with others; easily collaborating with another 符合的，一致的；和谐的

Louis and I were *congruent* in our thinking, so we worked well together on the science project. 路易斯和我想法很一致，因此我们在科学项目上合作很好。

adverb: **congruently**
noun: **congruence**

▶ **convivial**
/kən'vɪvɪəl/
a.

pleasant; fun to be with; sociable and friendly 欢乐的；友好的

As people started introducing themselves and sharing stories with one another, the party developed a *convivial* atmosphere. 人们开始相互介绍并与他人分享自己的故事，因此派对充满了欢乐的气氛。

adverb: **convivially**
noun: **conviviality**

▶ **cordial**
/'kɔrdʒəl/
a.

warm, sincere, friendly, and gracious 热诚的，友好的

The receptionist in the lobby was *cordial* when we asked her for information. 当我们向大厅的招待员咨询时，她很热情。

adverb: **cordially**
noun: **cordiality**

▶ **genial**
/'dʒinjəl/
a.

having a warm, friendly, and gracious nature 热情的，友好的，亲切的

Despite her initial barking, the dog had a most *genial* nature and simply wanted to be petted. 尽管这条狗开始时总叫，但本质上十分友好，只想受到宠爱。

adverb: **genially**
noun: **geniality**

▶ **harmonious** exhibiting a pleasant and easy demeanor; friendly and
/hɑr'monɪəs/ pleasant 和谐的，融洽的
a.

> Even though the household contained a cat, dog, bird, and
> fish, not to mention three teenagers, the home could usually
> boast a *harmonious* atmosphere. 虽然这家养了一只猫、
> 一条狗、一只鸟和一条鱼，更别提还有三个十几岁的孩子
> 了，但大家通常相处很和谐，气氛友好，并以此为荣。

adverb: **harmoniously**
noun: **harmony**

▶ **like-minded** of the same mind; in harmony with another 有相同想法的，
/ˌlaɪk'maɪdɪd/ 志趣相投的
a.

> The twins were so *like-minded* that they agreed on most issues.
> 这对双胞胎志趣相投，在大多数问题上都意见一致。

adverb: **like-mindedly**

▶ **obliging** ready to do favors for others; easy and willing to get along
/ə'blaɪdʒɪŋ/ with others 乐于助人的；易于相处的
a.

> My coworker was *obliging* about trading work shifts with
> me. 我的同事很热心，同意跟我换班。

adverb: **obligingly**
verb: **oblige**

··

▶ **aloof** distant physically or emotionally; reserved and remote; at a
/ə'luf/ distance but within view; apart 冷漠的，疏远的；远离的；
a. 分开的

Melissa was shy and seemed *aloof*, but that behavior was a defense against having to expose her timidity to others. 梅利莎很害羞，似乎也很冷漠，但她这样做是怕将自己的羞涩暴露给别人。

adverb: **aloofly**
noun: **aloofness**

▶ **arrogant**
/ˈærəgənt/
a.

having or displaying a sense of overbearing self-worth or self-importance 傲慢的，狂妄自大的

The *arrogant* media mogul acted as if she thought she was above the law. 这个传媒大亨举止傲慢，似乎觉得自己凌驾于法律之上。

adverb: **arrogantly**
noun: **arrogance**

▶ **contemptuous**
/kənˈtɛmptʃʊəs/
a.

manifesting or displaying strong dislike, scorn, or contempt 厌恶的，轻蔑的

The rising executive was so determined to climb the corporate ladder that he was *contemptuous* of the feelings of those he pushed aside so that he could advance. 这个受到提拔的主管一心想在公司往上爬，全然不顾那些被他视为有碍他发展的人的感受。

adverb: **contemptuously**
noun: **contemptuousness**

▶ **derisive**
/dɪˈraɪsɪv/
a.

mocking or scoffing 嘲笑的

Tom's *derisive* comment regarding the English teacher made it clear that he didn't think very highly of her. 汤姆对这个英语老师进行了一番嘲讽，这清楚地表明他对她的评价不高。

noun: **derision**
adverb: **derisively**

► **disdainful**
/dɪs'denfəl/
a.

demonstrating disdain, excessive pride, or scornful superiority
轻蔑的，鄙视的，不屑的

Lauren became so full of herself after being elected homecoming queen that her friends could no longer tolerate her *disdainful* attitude. 劳伦在被选为"校友聚会女王"之后变得很自大，她的朋友再也无法忍受她蔑视别人的态度了。

adverb: **disdainfully**
noun: **disdainfulness**

► **egocentric**
/ˌigo'sɛntrɪk/
a.

• behaving as if the entire world revolves around oneself; totally selfish 自我中心的；自私自利的

Because infants are incapable of doing anything for themselves and everyone else must respond to their needs and demands, they might be considered *egocentric*. 婴儿没有能力为自己做任何事，而其他的人必须去满足他们的需求，因此我们可以认为婴儿是以自我为中心的。

• a theory of philosophy in which one's own mind is the center of everything 利己主义的

Paula's belief in *egocentric* philosophies made her a very self-centered person. 葆拉拥护利己主义的信条，这使得她以自我为中心。

adverb: **egocentrically**
noun: **egocentric, egocentricity, egocentrism**

► **haughty**
/'hɔtɪ/

being overwhelmingly proud, vain, and self-centered 倨傲不逊的，以自我为中心的

a.　Siamese cats tend to be aloof, and some people consider them too ***haughty*** to be good pets. 暹罗猫往往很冷漠，所以有些人认为这些猫太傲慢而不能成为好的宠物。

adverb: **haughtily**
noun: **haughtiness**

▶**incongruous** inconsistent; inappropriate; not correct or customary
/ɪnˈkʌŋɡrʊəs/ according to the circumstances 前后矛盾的；不适当的；
a.　不协调的，不一致的

It was ***incongruous*** to see Chaltu at the student council meeting after she had been so openly critical of the council's decisions in the past. 查尔图如此公开地批评了学生自治会的决定之后，又出席了学生自治会的会议，这让人感觉前后矛盾。

adverb: **incongruously**
noun: **incongruity**

▶**pompous** displaying an exaggerated degree of dignity and self-
/ˈpʌmpəs/ importance 自高自大的，自负的
a.

The ***pompous*** customer said to the waiter, "I don't drink anything but bottled water from France." 自负的顾客对服务员说："除了法国瓶装水之外我什么都不喝。"

adverb: **pompously**
noun: **pompousness**

▶**priggish** displaying an overly affected or smug narrow-mindedness
/ˈprɪɡɪʃ/ 自负的
a.

Sally was so caught up in her own self-importance that people started referring to her as being ***priggish***. 由于萨莉深信自己很重要，人们开始认为她很自负。

adverb: **priggishly**

noun: **prig**

▶ **reticent**
/ˈrɛtəsn̩t/
a.

exceptionally restrained or reserved in mannerism or speech
沉默寡言的，言谈举止有保留的

Because Alfredo was afraid he would say something stupid,
he was *reticent* about joining the class discussion. 阿尔弗雷
多害怕自己会说出什么蠢话，因此不愿参与课堂讨论。

adverb: **reticently**

noun: **reticence**

▶ **sanctimonious**
/ˌsæŋktəˈmonɪəs/
a.

displaying excessive piety or a holier-than-thou attitude
假装虔诚的，假装圣洁的

Trying to impress his girlfriend's parents, Jack put on a
sanctimonious performance, even going to church with the
family although he was a professed atheist. 尽管杰克公开
宣称自己是无神论者，但为了打动他女朋友的父母，他
假装很虔诚，甚至和他们一家一起去教堂做礼拜。

adverb: **sanctimoniously**

noun: **sanctimony**

▶ **self-
aggrandizing**
/ˌsɛlf-
əˈgrændaɪzɪŋ/
a.

enhancing or exaggerating one's own importance, power, or
reputation 自我夸大的

Caught up in his new position as supervisor, Steve exhibited
self-aggrandizing behavior, which was not appreciated by
the staff who had to listen to his boasting. 史蒂夫认为监督
员这一新职位很了不起，因而自吹自擂，让那些不得不
听他自夸的员工感到讨厌。

noun: **self-aggrandizement**

▶ **self-righteous**
/ˌsɛlfˈraɪtʃəs/

overly sure of one's moral convictions or pious position
自以为是的，自以为正直善良的

a. The early American preacher Jonathan Edwards is known for his *self-righteous* sermon, "Sinners in the Hands of an Angry God." 美国早期传教士乔纳森 · 爱德华兹因其自以为是的训诫"罪人在愤怒的上帝手中"而出名。

noun: **self-righteousness**

▶ **self-satisfied** possessing satisfaction with oneself or one's accomplishments
/ˌsɛlfˈsætɪsfaɪd/ 自我满足的
a.

After winning the election, Veronica felt *self-satisfied* with her efforts. 赢得选举后，韦罗妮卡对自己的努力很满意。

noun: **self-satisfaction**

▶ **smug** being self-satisfied; complacent with oneself 自满的；自鸣得
/smʌɡ/ 意的
a.

Martha was obviously *smug* when she was the only student able to answer the teacher's question correctly. 玛莎是唯一一个能正确回答出老师问题的学生，显然她很自得。

adverb: **smugly**
noun: **smugness**

▶ **supercilious** displaying an overabundance of pride or vanity; extremely
/ˌsupɚˈsɪliəs/ smug or pleased with oneself 高傲的；自满的，洋洋自得的
a.

Roger was spoiled by doting grandparents who gave him everything, and he took *supercilious* pleasure in owning toys that his friends' families could not afford. 罗杰的祖父母什么东西都肯给他，他被他们宠坏了，因而他对家里买不起玩具的朋友有一种傲慢的愉悦感。

adverb: **superciliously**
noun: **superciliousness**

Sentence Completion 完成句子

Circle the word or word pair that best completes the meaning of the sentence. 圈出最符合句子含义的词或一对词。

1. Ralph was always ready to preach his beliefs to others, and his _____ got on everyone's nerves.
   A. complaisance
   B. sanctimony
   C. reticence
   D. pompousness
   E. aloofness

2. Because he had stuttered all his life, Paul was _____ about signing up for a speech class when he got to college.
   A. supercilious
   B. smug
   C. aloof
   D. reticent
   E. complaisant

3. Nancy _____ preached her personal beliefs, feeling certain that her convictions were correct.
   A. smugly
   B. superciliously
   C. arrogantly
   D. haughtily
   E. self-righteously

4. The _____ professor, considering himself above such menial tasks, would not answer his own phone, even when he was closer to it than the nearest servant.

A. pompous

B. reticent

C. self-righteous

D. smug

E. aloof

5. Being _____ and _____, the actress quickly dropped all her friends after she made her first successful movie.

A. egocentric/aloof

B. complaisant/haughty

C. arrogant/disdainful

D. reticent/priggish

E. supercilious/sanctimonious

Quick Matching 快速配对

Write the letter of the definition shown in the right column next to the word that matches it in the left column. 在右栏中找出与左栏单词相符的定义，将对应的字母写在单词旁。

_____1. affable   A. well-matched

_____2. self-aggrandizing B. expressing strong dislike

_____3. contemptuous   C. reserved in manner

_____4. reticent   D. pleasing to be with

_____5. compatible   E. enhancing or exaggerating one's own importance

Complete the Story 完成故事

Using these words selected from this unit, fill in the blanks to complete the story. 用本单元的词汇填空，完成故事。

unobliging	disdainful
self-satisfied	haughty
accommodating	contemptuous
smugly	reticent
arrogant	supercilious

In the late 1300s in England, Richard II was king. He was far from being an _____ monarch. In fact, he was _____ very _____ in response to his subjects' needs. Consequently, during his reign, the peasants were not _____ about letting the king know of their discontent. Led by Wat Tyler, they tried to revolt. The young king, not tolerant of such action, was _____ and unsympathetic to the peasants' cause. He believed he was king by divine right, and his _____ attitude caused many people to hate him. Nevertheless, he felt very _____ about his position, _____ reminding the peasants that they would never be able to become more than what they were — peasants. Although he was able to subdue the Peasants' Revolt, he was so _____ that this attitude alienated even those who supported his royal position. While he was out of the country, his kingship was overthrown, and, upon returning, he was put into prison. His _____ attitude did not go over well there, and he was assassinated while in captivity.

ANSWERS 答案

Sentence Completion 完成句子： 1-B, 2-D, 3-A, 4-A, 5-E

Quick Matching 快速配对： 1-D, 2-E, 3-B, 4-C, 5-A

Complete the Story 完成故事： accommodating, haughty, unobliging, reticent, disdainful, supercilious, self-satisfied, smugly, arrogant, contemptuous

Give or Receive
给予还是接受

有些人似乎天生慷慨而乐于助人——只要你提出来，他们的东西就会归你所有。相反，也有些人非常吝啬，不那么愿意和别人分享。同样，有些人既可以被视为十分慷慨，也会被视为十分吝啬——这往往取决于当局者自己的感觉。

abstemious	meager	parsimonious
chintzy	mercenary	penurious
closefisted	miserly	provident
frugal	niggardly	stingy

....

altruistic	lavish	philanthropy
benevolent	magnanimous	selfless
bounteously	munificent	self-sacrificing
eleemosynary	openhandedly	unstinting

► **abstemious**
/əb'stimɪəs/

a.

• eating or drinking in moderation 饮食有度的

The Puritans in colonial America were known for their *abstemious* way of life; not only did they refrain from excessive eating and drinking, but their everyday living was restricted to bare necessities. 美国殖民地时期，清教徒因其节俭的生活方式而闻名。他们饮食有所节制，日常用品仅仅是最基本的生活必需品。

• restricted to bare necessities; simplified 节俭的，有节制的，克制的

Their everyday life was so *abstemious* that the theaters were closed and the only social entertainment took place at lunch. 他们的日常生活十分节俭，很少去剧院以致剧院都关了门，午餐是唯一的社交娱乐活动时间。

adverb: **abstemiously**
noun: **abstemiousness**

► **chintzy**
/'tʃɪntsɪ/

a.

• gaudy or tacky 俗气的，廉价劣质的

The woman's red plastic purse looked *chintzy* in contrast to her designer cocktail dress. 这个女人的红色塑料钱包跟她的由专门设计师设计的短裙相比很俗气。

• miserly; tightfisted; stingy 吝啬的

In Charles Dickens's *A Christmas Carol*, Ebenezer Scrooge was so uncaring and *chintzy* that he thought he was doing Bob Cratchit a favor by letting him spend Christmas Day with his family. 查尔斯·狄更斯的《圣诞颂歌》一书中，埃比尼泽·斯克鲁奇冷漠而吝啬，他认为让鲍勃·克拉奇特圣诞节时和家人团聚是莫大的恩惠。

noun: **chintz**

► **closefisted**
/'klos'fɪstɪd/
a.

unwilling to part with money; sometimes known as hardfisted or tightfisted 吝啬的，小气的

In fact, Scrooge was so ***closefisted*** that he suggested giving Cratchit only half his pay for the one day a year the man had away from his job. 事实上，斯克鲁奇特吝啬到就连克拉奇特一年中唯一一天的休假他都只愿付给他半天的工资。

► **frugal**
/'frugl̩/
a.

costing or spending little; sparing in cost or expenditure 花费少的，节俭的

After my uncle lost his job, there was money only for bare necessities, so his entire family had to become much more ***frugal***. 叔叔失业后，家里的钱仅能购置最基本的生活必需品了。于是家人不得不更加节俭。

adverb: **frugally**
noun: **frugality, frugalness**

► **meager**
/'migɚ/
a.

scanty; deficient in quantity or extent; less than necessary 缺乏的，不足的

Because of the terrible weather during the prime growing season, the harvest was too ***meager*** to feed all the members of the tribe. 由于在庄稼生长季节初期天气恶劣，收成惨淡得无法喂饱族里所有的人。

adverb: **meagerly**
noun: **meagerness**

► **mercenary**
/'mɝsn̩ˌɛrɪ/
a.,n.

adjective: motivated only by monetary or personal gain 为钱的，图利的

Tobe had ***mercenary*** motives when she visited her rich aunt; she figured the elderly woman would leave her something in her will. 托布去看望有钱的姑姑是为了钱。她觉得这个

上了年纪的人在遗嘱中肯定会分自己一份财产。

noun: a person who hires himself or herself out to fight for a foreign army 雇佣兵

Many French Huguenots fought in the American Revolution as *mercenaries*; some fought on the side of the Colonies, and some for the British. 许多法国胡格诺派教徒作为雇佣兵参加了美国独立战争。有些站在殖民地一边，有些则为英国而战。

▶**miserly**
/'maɪzɚlɪ/
a.

stingy and sparing; not generous or willing to share or to be sympathetic to the plight of others 极其吝啬的

Never one to share his good fortune with others, Roscoe was so *miserly* that he cut all his family members out of his will. 从来不愿把财产分给他人的罗斯科，吝啬到在遗嘱中没有提到任何一个家庭成员。

noun: **miser, miserliness**

▶**niggardly**
/'nɪgɚdlɪ/
a.

stingy and miserly; not willing to part with anything, especially money (This word comes from the Scandinavian *nig*, meaning a stingy person.) 小气的，吝啬的（该词来源于斯堪的纳维亚语的nig一词，表示吝啬的人）

Thelma was so *niggardly* about money that she thought a twenty-five cent tip was more than enough to leave to the hard-working server who had served her a $15 dinner. 特尔玛花钱很小气。她晚餐花了15美元，但却认为给为她辛勤服务的侍者25美分已足够多了。

▶**parsimonious** excessively sparing or frugal, cautious about any sort
/ˌpɑrsə'monɪəs/ of spending 过分节俭的
a.

Serge's friends were embarrassed by his *parsimonious*

behavior, so they often paid for everything rather than have him count pennies all the time. 瑞奇的朋友都为他的过分节俭而难堪，因此他们宁愿去买单，也不会让他锱铢必较，耿耿于怀。

noun: **parsimoniousness**
adverb: **parsimoniously**

▶**penurious**
/pəˈnʊriəs/
a.

- unwilling to spend or spare any money 不愿花钱的
- unyielding, unprofitable 无产出的，不获利的
- poverty-stricken 贫困的

The man was so ***penurious*** that he asked his children to help him pay for groceries. 这个人贫困到要他的孩子为他支付买食品杂物的钱。

adverb: **penuriously**
noun: **penuriousness, penury**

▶**provident**
/ˈprɑvədənt/
a.

- careful and circumspect in one's behavior, especially concerning the future 有远见的
- careful when spending money 节俭的
- careful to look out for one's own interests 深谋远虑的

Even when he was ***provident*** with his money, he never had enough to get him through each week. 尽管他生活很节俭，但每周都入不敷出。

noun: **providence**
adverb: **providently**

▶**stingy**
/ˈstɪndʒɪ/
a.

- a common term describing someone who is tightfisted or miserly 吝啬的，小气的
- unyielding such as in barrenness in land or productivity 无产出的，（土地）贫瘠的

Reluctant to help him out, however, his *stingy* children humiliated the old man by making him beg for every penny they gave him. 然而，老人吝啬的孩子们很不情愿帮助他，他们刻意羞辱他，让他为得到每一分钱而祈求施舍。

noun: **stinginess**
adverb: **stingily**

....

▶**altruistic**
/ˌæltruˈɪstɪk/
a.

truly generous and not concerned with self but concerned rather with the welfare of others 利他的，无私的

The retired man was fortunate to come across a very successful old friend whose *altruistic* nature made him only too willing to help his old comrade. 这个退休老人很幸运地遇到了一个事业很成功的老朋友。老朋友天生一副热心肠，很愿意帮助他的老战友。

adverb: **altruistically**
noun: **altruism**

▶**benevolent**
/bəˈnɛvələnt/
a.

having goodwill and generosity, especially toward those less fortunate 仁慈的，乐善好施的

This *benevolent* friend was so easy-mannered that he never made the retired man feel the least bit embarrassed by his situation. 这位乐善好施的朋友为人随和，从不让他已退休的好朋友为自己的境遇感到难堪。

adverb: **benevolently**
noun: **benevolence**

▶**bounteously**
/ˈbaʊntɪəslɪ/
ad.

generously and copiously (in ample quantities) given 慷慨地，大方地

In fact, this rich friend shared his good fortune so ***bounteously*** that the retired man was able to pay back his children and not have to feel humiliated ever again. 事实上，这个富有的朋友慷慨地与退休老人分享了他的财产，使得退休老人有能力偿还孩子们的钱，再也不用感到羞辱了。

adjective: **bounteous**
noun: **bounteousness**

▶**eleemosynary** generously given; benevolent (comes from the Latin,
/ˌɛləˈmɑsn̩ɛrɪ/ related to the word *alms*, money given to the poor) 施舍的，
a. 慈善的（该词来源于拉丁文，与alms相关联，指施舍给穷人的钱）

The retired man felt that he could never properly repay the ***eleemosynary*** generosity of his friend, but his friend reminded him that their friendship was worth more than anything money could ever buy. 退休老人对于朋友的乐善好施无以为报，但朋友说他们之间的友谊比钱更珍贵。

▶**lavish** • extravagant and profuse 浪费的；极多的
/ˈlævɪʃ/
a. Miriam is a ***lavish*** hostess; nothing is too good or too much for her houseguests. 米丽娅姆是个毫不吝啬的女主人。招待来客的饭菜非常可口，量也极大。

• willing to give generously, often excessively 过分慷慨的

The young bride planned a ***lavish*** wedding reception at which the food averaged about $120 per guest. 这个年轻的新娘计划了一场奢华的婚宴，平均每位来宾花费120美元。

adverb: **lavishly**
noun: **lavishness**

▶**magnanimous** • courageous and noble in heart and mind 高尚的，勇敢的
/mæɡ'nænəməs/
a.

Sir Lancelot, although he loved Guinevere, was a *magnanimous* knight who respected the fact that she was Arthur's wife. 尽管兰斯洛特爱着吉尼维尔，但作为一个高尚的骑士他尊重吉尼维尔是亚瑟的妻子这一事实。

• generous; willing to share one's bounty with others 慷慨的

The father of the bride was a likable person with a *magnanimous* spirit, so all the guests felt welcome and comfortable around him. 新娘的父亲是个慷慨而和蔼可亲的人，因此客人们都觉得跟他在一起很随意、很舒服。

adverb: **magnanimously**
noun: **magnanimity**

▶**munificent** showing great generosity, often in a regal or princely manner
/mju'nɪfəsṇt/ 慷慨的，大方的
a.

The bride was fortunate to have a rich and *munificent* father who gave her whatever she wanted. 这个新娘十分幸运，她的父亲富有而慷慨，她要什么父亲就给什么。

adverb: **munificently**
noun: **munificence**

▶**openhandedly** liberally, generously, and freely bestowing upon others 慷
/ˌopən'hændɪdlɪ/ 慨的，（出手）大方的
a.

In fact, the reception was so excessive that the bride *openhandedly* gave each of the guests an expensive memento. 事实上，婚宴极为奢华，新娘出手大方，送给每一位来宾一个很贵重的纪念品。

adjective: **openhanded**

noun: **openhandedness**

▶**philanthropy** goodwill; effort to promote human welfare 慈善
/fə'lænθrəpɪ/

n. Because of this father's ***philanthropy*** toward the city's chamber orchestra, the musicians were more than happy to play at his daughter's wedding reception. 由于父亲对市里的室内管弦乐队的慈善之举，音乐家们都十分乐意为他女儿的婚宴演出。

adverb: **philanthropically**
adjective: **philanthropic**

▶**selfless** not motivated by any concern for self, only for others; unselfish
/'sɛlflɪs/ 无私的，忘我的

a.

In order to be a good police officer or firefighter, one must be truly ***selfless***, often putting oneself in danger in order to care for or protect others. 要想做一名好警官或者好消防员，必须要无私奉献，为保护他人的利益而把自身的安危置之度外。

adverb: **selflessly**
noun: **selflessness**

▶**self-sacrificing** totally unselfish; willing to go beyond the norm to give to
/ˌsɛlf'sækrəfaɪsɪŋ/ others 无私的，自我牺牲的

a.

Much of this ***self-sacrificing*** character was evident in those who helped during and after the 9/11 attack. "9•11" 恐怖袭击事件发生当时及事过之后，自我牺牲的精神在很多助人者身上体现了出来。

adverb: **self-sacrificingly**

▶**unstinting** • marked by lavish overabundance 极为大方的，无限制的
/ʌn'stɪntɪŋ/

a.

Charles was an ***unstinting*** suitor: He sent Valerie flowers and gifts all the time. 查尔斯是个极其大方的求婚者——他总是不停地给瓦莱丽送去鲜花和礼物。

• **bestowed upon liberally, with much devotion and even self-sacrifice** 有奉献精神的，有牺牲精神的

Hour upon hour, firefighters from New York and many from outside the city were ***unstinting*** in their efforts to recover survivors from the World Trade Center wreckage. 一小时又一小时过去了，纽约及许多从城外赶来的消防员忘我地工作，努力地寻找世贸大楼废墟下的幸存者。

adverb: **unstintingly**

Sentence Completion 完成句子

Circle the word or word pair that best completes the meaning of the sentence. 圈出最符合句子含义的词或一对词。

1. Jonah's father was so _____ that during college Jonah had to hold two jobs in order to make ends meet.
   A. stingy
   B. penurious
   C. lavish
   D. benevolent
   E. altruistic

2. Pamela disliked the poorly made dress; she thought it looked _____.
   A. closefisted
   B. lavish
   C. chintzy
   D. munificent
   E. abstemious

3. Sasha was so _____ in her behavior that she was always helping others _____.
   A. openhanded/penuriously
   B. lavish/providentially
   C. provident/abstemiously
   D. bounteous/niggardly
   E. self-sacrificing/selflessly

4. Isaac's _____ personal spending enabled him to practice _____ for many worthy causes.
   A. stingy/selflessness
   B. unstinting/bounteousness
   C. meager/lavishness
   D. altruistic/frugality
   E. self-sacrificing/munificence

5. Rachel _____ delivered food to the needy during the holidays; she acted _____, never expecting anything in return for her generous spirit.
   A. openhandedly/magnanimously
   B. philanthropically/selflessly
   C. meagerly/frugally
   D. benevolently/abstemiously
   E. lavishly/unstintingly

Quick Matching 快速配对

Write the letter of the definition shown in the right column next to the word that matches it in the left column. 在右栏中找出与左栏单词相符的定义，将对应的字母写在单词旁。

_____ 1. altruistic	A. miserly
_____ 2. lavish	B. careful
_____ 3. provident	C. unstinting
_____ 4. parsimonious	D. bounteous
_____ 5. niggardly	E. frugal

Complete the Story 完成故事

Using these words selected from this unit, fill in the blanks to complete the story. 用本单元的词汇填空，完成故事。

meager	selflessly
frugal	parsimonious
openhanded	philanthropy
self-sacrificing	lavish
stingy	benevolent
magnanimous	abstemious
chintzy	unstinting
miserly	closefisted

Visiting my father's parents and visiting my mother's parents is a study in opposites. Overall, my father's family is very _____; none of them is willing to spend an extra dime on anything. In fact, they are so _____ and _____ that they often buy things of _____ quality that look cheap and _____. My grandfather is so _____ about every purchase that family get-togethers are far from _____. Even Thanksgiving dinners are quite _____. He acknowledges this character trait, however, and even he laughs at his own _____ spending behavior.

In contrast, my mother's family are the most generous and _____ people you'll ever meet. Every family gathering is _____ in food and drink. My mother's father is very _____; he always slips each grandchild $5 or $10. His generosity is also public; his _____ is often demonstrated by his _____ donations to the arts and to education. He's a _____ person who _____ not only gives his money but volunteers his time and services as well.

ANSWERS 答案

Sentence Completion 完成句子：1-A, 2-C, 3-E, 4-E, 5-B

Quick Matching 快速配对：1-C, 2-D, 3-B, 4-E, 5-A

Complete the Story 完成故事：frugal, stingy, miserly, meager, chintzy, parsimonious, lavish, abstemious, closefisted, benevolent, unstinting, openhanded, philanthropy, magnanimous, self-sacrificing, selflessly

Commend or Condemn
称赞还是谴责

每天我们都能从新闻里听到可怕的事件，新闻评论员总会对责任承担者极尽谴责。他们公开*指责*（*denounce*）应受谴责的（*reprehensible*）行为——一些公众人物理应成为公众的模范，但他们的行为却*应受指责*（*blameworthy*），新闻评论员对他们的评论也是*贬损的*（*disparaging*）。在我们的语言里，似乎没有足够的词汇来报道这类*应受谴责的*（*deplorable*）事件。

另一方面，新闻偶尔也对一些*值得赞扬的*（*creditable*）成就进行褒赞，*颂扬*（*extol*）那些*值得赞扬的*（*praiseworthy*）、令人赞美的（*laudable*）事迹。下列单词给我们提供了丰富的资源用来赞美和谴责。

acclaim	creditable	laudable
admirable	encomium	meritorious
applaud	esteem	panegyric
approbation	eulogy	praiseworthy
celebrate	extol	
citation	kudos	

abominate	culpable	disparage
admonitory	decry	excoriate
berate	denounce	objurgate
blameworthy	deplore	reprehensible
castigate	deprecate	reproachful
censurable	despise	reprove

▶ **acclaim**
/ə'klem/
v., n.

verb: to applaud or congratulate with much enthusiasm; to strongly approve 欢呼，喝彩；赞同

The coach will always *acclaim* his team whenever they perform well. 只要球队表现得好，教练都会为他们鼓掌喝彩。

noun: enthusiastic applause or recognition 欢呼，称赞

The Olympic gold medal skater was met with much *acclaim* when he returned to his small native country. 当这个在奥运会上获得金牌的滑冰运动员回到自己的小国时，迎接他的是狂热的欢呼。

noun: **acclamation**
adjective: **acclaimed**

▶ **admirable**
/'ædmərəbl̩/
a.

worthy of being admired or respected 令人钦佩的，令人尊重的

Patrick's behavior was *admirable*; when the little girl ran in front of the car, he ran into the street and picked her up, saving her from probable disaster. 帕特里克的行为令人钦佩：当小女孩跑到汽车前时，他冲上去抱起了她，避免了一场悲剧的发生。

verb: **admire**
adverb: **admirably**
noun: **admirability**

▶ **applaud**
/ə'plɔd/
v.

to express approval, often by the clapping of hands 鼓掌；称赞

The high school principal *applauded* the teacher's quick response when a student had a seizure in her classroom. 事后，中学校长为这个老师在课堂上突遇学生发病时的快速反应而表示赞许。

adjective: **applaudable**

noun: **applauder, applause**

adverb: **applaudably**

▶ **approbation** expression of approval, often official in nature [正式]称
/ˌæprəˈbeʃən/ 赞，认可，批准
n.

> The mayor's ***approbation*** for solving the difficult case was helpful to the police department, which had been receiving negative publicity. 市长对于破获这个疑难案件所给予的认可与赞赏给了警方很大帮助，因为一直以来警方为负面舆论所困扰。

verb: **approbate**

adjective: **approbative, approbatory**

▶ **celebrate** • to praise or make widely known or creditable 颂扬，赞美
/ˈsɛləˌbret/
v.

> The family ***celebrated*** Shawna's success when she won a National Merit Scholarship. 肖娜获得了国家优秀学生奖学金，家人都向她表示祝贺。

• to observe certain seasons or festivities 庆祝（节日）

> During fall and early winter many cultures ***celebrate*** a variety of religious holidays. 秋末冬初时，许多文化都会庆祝各种各样的宗教节日。

noun: **celebration**

adjective: **celebratory**

▶ **citation** official commendation or recognition 嘉奖
/saɪˈteʃən/
n.

> Moira received a ***citation*** for her exemplary behavior in a critical situation. 莫伊拉因她在关键时刻的表率行为赢得

了嘉奖。

adjective: **citational**

▶ **creditable**
/'krɛdɪtəbl̩/
a.

• deserving of often limited praise 值得称赞的

His performance at the talent show was not the best he'd ever given, but it was *creditable*. 他在才艺大赛上的表现尽管并不是他的最高水平，但仍然是值得称赞的。

• deserving of commercial credit or reputation 值得给予商业贷款的，有商业信誉的

Her supervisor told Sam that the new vendor was a *creditable* company, worthy of pursuing. 萨姆的主管告诉她说，这个新的卖主是一家有信誉的公司，可以与之合作。

noun: **credit**
adverb: **creditably**

▶ **encomium**
/ɛn'komɪəm/
n.

warm, deserving praise; a tribute 高度赞扬，赞颂；赞词

The squad commander gave the soldier an *encomium* for his brave and selfless action that saved three other lives. 班长高度赞扬了这位士兵，正是因为他的英勇和无私救了其他三人。

▶ **esteem**
/ə'stim/
n.

favorable respect or regard 尊敬，好评

The learned professor was held in such *esteem* that his classes were always the first to fill at registration. 这位博学的教授备受推崇，他的课总是在第一时间就给报满了。

adjective: **estimable**
noun: **estimation**
verb: **esteem**

▶ **eulogy**
/ˈjuːlədʒɪ/
n.

a laudatory speech written in praise of a person, usually after his or her death 颂词，颂文（尤指葬礼上的悼词和悼文）

At the senator's funeral, several people gave *eulogies* mentioning his accomplishments. 在该参议员的葬礼上，一些人在颂词中肯定了他所取得的成就。

verb: **eulogize**
adjective: **eulogistic**

▶ **extol**
/ɪkˈstol/
v.

to praise highly 高度赞美，颂扬

The townspeople *extolled* the world-renowned hero when he returned to his home. 当这位享誉世界的英雄荣归故里时，市民们啧啧称赞。

noun: **extoller, extolment**

▶ **kudos**
/ˈkjuːdɑs/
n.

praise; a compliment 荣誉，名声，威信

Kudos go to the employee who came up with this innovative and practical suggestion. 该员工提出这一具有创造性、操作性强的建议，值得赞赏。

▶ **laudable**
/ˈlɔːdəbl̩/
a.

worthy of praise and/or recognition 值得赞美的

Although his accomplishment was *laudable*, the man was humble in accepting the mayor's congratulations. 尽管他的成就很值得赞美，但他在接受市长祝贺时依然十分谦恭。

noun: **laudableness, laudability**
adverb: **laudably**

▶ **meritorious**　deserving of award, merit, or praise 值得奖励的，值得称
/ˌmɛrəˈtɔːrɪəs/　赞的

a.   During the aftermath of the 9/11 tragedy, many firefighters and police officers demonstrated *meritorious* behavior that made Americans proud. "9·11"悲剧发生后，许多消防员和警察的表现值得赞扬，令美国人民为之骄傲。

adverb: **meritoriously**
noun: **merit**

▶ **panegyric**   a formal public compliment or elaborate praise 颂词，颂文
/ˌpænəˈdʒɪrɪk/

n.   After all the statesman had done for his home state, there was much *panegyric* upon the news of his unexpected death. 得知该政治家意外死亡的消息，人们纷纷撰文纪念他为国家所做出的贡献。

adjective: **panegyrical**
adverb: **panegyrically**

▶ **praiseworthy**   meriting praise and high commendation 值得赞扬的，可嘉许的
/ˈprezˌwɜðɪ/
a.

For 10 years in a row Isabel demonstrated *praiseworthy* behavior when she missed out on having dinner with her family in order to serve Thanksgiving dinner to the needy at the soup kitchen. 连续十年以来，伊莎贝尔割舍了与家人共进晚餐的机会，来到施舍处为穷人提供感恩节晚餐，这种表现是值得称赞的。

adverb: **praiseworthily**
noun: **praiseworthiness**

· ·

▶ **abominate**   to detest thoroughly 憎恨，厌恶
/əˈbɑːməˌnet/

v.   Cinderella's stepsisters *abominated* her to the extent that they did everything they could to prevent her from attending the prince's ball. 灰姑娘的同父异母姐妹对她的憎恶到了

极致——她们用尽一切手段阻止她参加王子的舞会。

adjective: **abominable**
noun: **abomination**
adverb: **abominably**

▶**admonitory** mildly cautionary, reproving, or scolding 告诫的，轻责的
/əd'mɑnəˌtɔrɪ/

a.　　My mother's ***admonitory*** tone let me know that she was unhappy with me, even though her words were not harsh. 母亲告诫的口吻让我明白了她的不悦，尽管她的言语并不犀利。

noun: **admonition**
verb: **admonish**

▶**berate** to scold angrily and at length 严责，训斥
/bɪ'ret/

v.　　Sean's mother was constantly ***berating*** him for keeping his room so messy. 肖恩的母亲总是责备他把房子弄得一团糟。

▶**blameworthy** worthy of blame or reproof; guilty; deserving punishment
/'blemˌwɝðɪ/　应受责备的；有过失的；应受惩罚的
a.

Since my friends and I had been playing ball in the yard, we were ***blameworthy*** when the ball shattered our neighbor's large front window. 我和朋友在院子里踢球的时候不小心踢碎了邻居家前窗的大玻璃，对此我们是应受责备的。

noun: **blameworthiness**

▶**castigate** to criticize thoroughly, even to punish for an infraction 严
/'kæstəˌget/ 厉责骂；严惩
v.

After I broke the window, my father ***castigated*** me soundly and grounded me for a month. 我踢碎了窗户之后，父亲狠狠地教训了我一顿，并且一个月不让我出去和朋友玩。

noun: **castigation**

▶ **censurable**
/'sɛnʃərəbl̩/

deserving of censure or blame 应受谴责的

a.　The *censurable* behavior of the sociopath Ted Bundy horrified the public. 连环杀人犯特德·邦迪应受谴责的变态行为使公众感到恐慌。

verb: **censure**

▶ **culpable**
/'kʌlpəbl̩/

at fault; deserving blame 错误的；应受谴责的

a.　The crumbs stuck on his face made it easy to see that my little brother was *culpable* of raiding the cookie jar. 从弟弟脸上的糕饼屑不难看出他偷吃了饼干。

noun: **culpability, culpableness**
adverb: **culpably**

▶ **decry**
/dɪ'kraɪ/

to openly condemn 公开谴责

v.　The crowd loudly *decried* the traitor before he was executed. 人们在叛徒受刑前大声地谴责他。

noun: **decrier**

▶ **denounce**
/dɪ'naʊns/

to condemn, criticize, or accuse 谴责，批评，指控

v.　The court of King Henry VIII was quick to *denounce* Anne Boleyn as a traitor when Henry no longer wanted her as his wife. 亨利八世的朝臣在得知国王休掉皇后安妮·博林的企图之后，迅速将安妮指控为叛国者。

noun: **denouncement, denouncer, denunciation**

▶ **deplore**
/dɪ'plɔr/

to express strong dislike or disapproval; to condemn 强烈反对

v.　Joe *deplored* his brother's illegal actions; he always knew that his brother's friends would eventually lead him to trouble. 乔强烈反对他哥哥的非法行为。他明白哥哥的狐朋狗友最终会使哥哥陷入困境。

adjective: **deplorable**
adverb: **deplorably**

▶ **deprecate**　to belittle; express disapproval; deplore 贬低；反对；谴责
/'dɛprə,ket/

v.　The hockey player's *deprecating* tone toward the referee was not tolerated, and he soon found himself sitting in the penalty box. 曲棍球运动员对裁判表示了强烈不满，他很快就坐到了受罚席。

noun: **deprecation**
adjective: **deprecating**
adverb: **deprecatingly**

▶ **despise**　to look down on with contempt or scorn 藐视，鄙视
/dɪ'spaɪz/

v.

It was easy for Mary to *despise* her former friend after their argument. 有过争执之后，玛丽很容易对她这位以前的朋友心生鄙视。

adjective: **despicable**
adverb: **despicably**
noun: **despiser**

▶ **disparage**　to speak in a disrespectful way; to belittle; to reduce in
/dɪ'spærɪdʒ/　esteem 贬低；轻视

v.

It is not unusual for opposing forces to *disparage* one another during a closely contested election. 在一场势均力敌的竞选中，对手间互相诋毁的现象并不罕见。

noun: **disparagement, disparager**
adverb: **disparagingly**

▶ **excoriate**
/ɪkˈskɔrɪˌet/
v.

to censure severely; to denounce; to scold; to rebuke sharply 严厉批评，痛斥

After the public scandal, the press was quick to *excoriate* the congressman for his unethical behavior. 在该国会议员的丑闻暴露于众之后，媒体很快痛斥了他的不道德行为。

noun: **excoriation**

▶ **objurgate**
/ˈɑbdʒɚˌget/
v.

to scold sharply; to berate 痛骂，严斥

The judge was quick to *objurgate* the jury members when he found out that they had been watching television. 当发现陪审团成员一直在看电视时，法官就斥责了他们。

noun: **objurgation**
adverb: **objurgatorily**
adjective: **objurgatory**

▶ **reprehensible** deserving rebuke, scolding, or censure 应受谴责的
/ˌrɛprɪˈhɛnsəbl̩/
a.

The criminal's *reprehensible* behavior made it difficult for the defense lawyer to make much of an impression on the jury. 罪犯应受谴责的行为使得辩护律师很难说服陪审团。

noun: **reprehensibility**
adverb: **reprehensibly**

▶ **reproachful** deserving reproach or blame 应受责备的
/rɪˈprotʃfl̩/
a.

After Ed got in trouble, he felt that his parents were always giving him *reproachful* looks. 埃德惹上麻烦后，感到父

母总在用责备的眼神看他。

noun: **reproachfulness**
adverb: **reproachfully**

► **reprove**
/rɪ'pruv/
v.

to voice reproof or disapproval; to find fault with 不赞成；指责

Shana frequently *reproved* the homecoming committee for not getting its float built as quickly as it should have. 莎娜经常谴责返校节筹备委员会不按进度尽快建造花车。

noun: **reproval, reprover**
adjective: **reprovable**
adverb: **reprovingly**

Sentence Completion 完成句子

Circle the word or word pair that best completes the meaning of the sentence. 圈出最符合句子含义的词或一对词。

1. After returning from their successful mission, the four astronauts were given a presidential _____, which was televised nationwide.
   A. applause
   B. panegyric
   C. celebration
   D. denouncement
   E. disparagement

2. Henri was surprised by the principal's _____ tone because he knew that he was not responsible for what had happened and therefore not _____.
   A. admirable/creditable
   B. laudatory/laudable
   C. admonitory/blameworthy
   D. censurable/deplorable
   E. disparaging/esteemed

3. The Nobel Prize winner received national _____ and _____ for his incredible invention.
   A. acclaim/approbation
   B. applause/admonition
   C. abomination/approbation
   D. admiration/censure
   E. kudos/castigation

4. The biased talk show host _____ the congressman for his _____ behavior.

A. extolled/deplorable

B. decried/laudable

C. acclaimed/reproachful

D. castigated/reprehensible

E. reproved/meritorious

5. During the funeral ceremony, the Army commander _____ the dead soldier's _____ action in battle.

A. extolled/abominable

B. objurgated/praiseworthy

C. approbated/censurable

D. berated/deplorable

E. eulogized/meritorious

Quick Matching 快速配对

Write the letter of the definition shown in the right column next to the word that matches it in the left column. 在右栏中找出与左栏单词相符的定义，将对应的字母写在单词旁。

_____1. kudos   A. express approval

_____2. deplore   B. to openly condemn

_____3. decry   C. to scold

_____4. objurgate   D. praise and compliments

_____5. applaud   E. express disapproval

Complete the Story 完成故事

Using these words selected from this unit, fill in the blanks to complete the story. 用本单元的词汇填空，完成故事。

deplorable	excoriating
admirable	esteem
applaud	reprehensible
denounce	creditable
castigated	laudable
excoriate	celebrated
kudos	estimable

Recently, City Theater presented an atypical but _____ interpretation of Shakespeare's *Richard III*. Shakespeare's King Richard III is not an _____ character. In fact, historians generally _____ his selfish, some think traitorous, behavior and _____ actions. He was the hunchbacked, physically impaired king who supposedly had his two nephews killed because he saw them as a threat to his position as king. For this he has been universally _____. In addition, he had his brother drowned, supposedly in a vat of wine — another _____ act.

The local stage production, however, portrays Richard in a better light, much less _____ than history would have him. This production has created a Richard that makes the audience almost feel sorry for him. The audience actually develops a tendency to _____ his courage, not berate him. Rather than a hunchback, this Richard is handicapped, and he stumps about the stage on crutches. The nimble actor uses the crutches to his advantage, often swinging from them, vaulting onto a low wall, and even using them as a makeshift weapon. The actor's outstanding performance makes the audience _____ Richard for how he copes with his deformity. Through implication and a bit of poetic license with a few of Shakespeare's original lines, we quickly gather that he is a victim to be _____ for his amazing coping abilities. He is set up — someone other than he is responsible for the deaths—and the audience quickly understands that, without his _____ wits and strong survival instinct, he too might become a victim.

Needless to say, critics are mixed in their reactions to this production. The purists are quick to _____ the director as unprofessional and as only interested in making money while cheapening the original intent of the play. The more open-minded viewers, however, find this interpretation refreshing. They claim this new interpretation is _____ and offer many _____ to all those responsible for this original production.

ANSWERS 答案
Sentence Completion 完成句子: 1-B, 2-C, 3-A, 4-D, 5-E
Quick Matching 快速配对: 1-D, 2-E, 3-B, 4-C, 5-A
Complete the Story 完成故事: creditable, admirable, excoriate, reprehensible, castigated, deplorable, excoriating, esteem, applaud, celebrated, estimable, denounce, laudable, kudos

Fortitude or Foolhardiness
刚毅还是蛮勇

人们经常因为情况非常*危险*（*perilous*）而必须展现出勇气。由于英雄和莽夫有着明显的区别，我们有各种各样的词汇描写勇敢和*大胆*（*daring*）的行为。一个人很容易表现得很大胆，但实际上却是*蛮勇*（*foolhardiness*）。这些区别更多地取决于其他人的感觉而不是行为本身。

audacious	gallant	steadfast
bravado	intrepid	tenacious
dauntless	plucky	valiant
defiance	resolute	virago
fortitude	stalwart	

brash	hotheaded	offhanded
capricious	impetuous	perilous
daring	impulsive	rash
derring-do	insolent	reckless
foolhardy	madcap	temerity

►**audacious**
/ɔ'deʃəs/
a.

• fearlessly bold; possibly even foolhardy and daring 大胆的，无畏的；愚勇的

During the 9/11 tragedy, many ***audacious*** firemen gave their lives saving others. "9·11"事件中，许多英勇的消防员为了拯救他人而牺牲了自己的生命。

• unrestrained by convention or propriety; insolent 不受约束的，放肆的，无礼的

Emily displayed her ***audacious*** spirit when she arrived at the prom wearing a tuxedo. 埃米莉身着男士无尾礼服出现在舞会上，尽显她无拘无束的风格。

• spirited and original 大胆的，独创的

Hollywood producers did an ***audacious*** interpretation of Shakespeare's *Macbeth* when they made it into a gangster movie. 好莱坞制片人将莎士比亚的《麦克白》进行了大胆的演绎，将其改编成一部盗匪片。

noun: **audaciousness**
adverb: **audaciously**

►**bravado**
/brə'vɑdo/
n.

a tendency toward showy defiance or false expressions of courage 故作勇敢，虚张声势

Often soldiers must bolster their courage with showy displays of ***bravado*** in order to keep up their nerve. 战士们经常要通过夸张地展示自己的勇敢来给自己打气，以保持斗志。

►**dauntless**
/'dɔntlɪs/
a.

not easily intimidated; courageous and brave 无畏的，勇敢的

Many of the rescuers who worked at Ground Zero after 9/11 were ***dauntless*** in the face of danger and sorrow. "9·11"

事件发生后，许多工作在倒塌现场的援救者们在面对危险和悲伤时表现出英勇无畏的精神。

adverb: **dauntlessly**
noun: **dauntlessness**

▶**defiance**
/dɪˈfaɪəns/
n.

• bold resistance; brave opposition （公然）违抗；蔑视

Defiance was evident in the eyes of the young boy as he withstood taunting and teasing from his classmates. 面对那些奚落和嘲笑他的同学们，这个小男孩的眼里充满了不屑。

• arrogant attitude, often rude and dismissive. 藐视的态度，挑衅的态度

The disobedient child displayed his *defiance* when he stubbornly refused to obey his parents. 这个不听话的孩子固执地反抗父母的意愿，摆出一副挑衅的样子。

adjective: **defiant**
adverb: **defiantly**
verb: **defy**

▶**fortitude**
/ˈfɔːrtəˌtjuːd/
n.

showing great strength and bravery under adverse conditions such as pain and torture 坚韧，刚毅

Despite being grilled and tortured regularly by his captors, the POW colonel's *fortitude* kept him alive. 尽管这位被俘的上校经常被逮捕他的人盘问和折磨，但他凭借顽强的毅力活了下来。

▶**gallant**
/ˈɡælənt/
a.

• bold and dashing 大胆的；殷勤有礼的

The *gallant* Sir Walter Raleigh is said to have laid his cloak across a puddle so that Queen Elizabeth would not get her shoes wet as she walked by. 据说沃尔特·罗利爵士曾经殷勤地将他的斗篷铺在水坑上，以免伊丽莎白女王路过时弄湿了鞋子。

• bravely daring; selflessly courageous 无畏的，英勇的

The soldiers at the battle of the Alamo made a *gallant* attempt to save the fort from their attackers, but not one of them managed to survive. 阿拉莫战役中，战士们不惧敌人的攻击英勇地坚守要塞，但最终无一幸存。

• stately; majestic; seemingly regal in demeanor 宏伟的，堂皇的

When the *Titanic* sailed from Queensland, Ireland, no one would have predicted that such a grand and *gallant* ship would suffer such a disastrous ending. 当"泰坦尼克"号驶出爱尔兰昆士兰州时，没人会预料到如此富丽堂皇的巨轮会遭遇毁灭性的结局。

noun: **gallantry**
adverb: **gallantly**

▶ **intrepid**
/ɪnˈtrɛpɪd/
a.

courageous; acting with much determination and little fear 无畏的，勇敢的

Neil Armstrong, the first man to walk on the moon, was an *intrepid* pioneer of the twentieth century. 尼尔·阿姆斯特朗作为第一个在月球上行走的人，是20世纪勇敢的先锋者代表。

noun: **intrepidity, intrepidness**
adverb: **intrepidly**

▶ **plucky**
/ˈplʌkɪ/

having or displaying courage, tenacity, and resourcefulness under difficult or trying circumstances （面对困境）有勇

a.　气的，有胆量的

After the accident that resulted in paralysis of most of his body, Christopher Reeve has demonstrated his *plucky* approach to life and his own handicap by turning his misfortune into a campaign to support research into paralysis. 在一场导致他身体大部分瘫痪的事故后，克里斯托弗·里夫向世人展示了他坚定的生活信念和敢于面对残疾的勇气，以自身的不幸呼吁社会对瘫痪病症的关注和研究。

noun: **pluck, pluckiness**
adverb: **pluckily**

▶ **resolute**
/'rɛzəˌlut/
a.

firm, determined, and unwavering 坚定的，果断的

Martha was *resolute* in her determination to lose 10 pounds before the prom. 玛莎果断地决定舞会前减掉10磅体重。

adverb: **resolutely**
noun: **resolution**
verb: **resolve**

▶ **stalwart**
/'stɔlwɚt/
a.

strong, bold, daring, firm, and resolute; having determination and a stick-to-it attitude 强健的；勇敢的；坚定的

Though his actions were foolish, Don Quixote was a determined and *stalwart* pursuer of his dreams. 尽管堂·吉诃德行为有些愚蠢，但他是个坚定不移的追梦者。

adverb: **stalwartly**
noun: **stalwartness**

▶ **steadfast**
/'stɛdˌfæst/
a.

steady and reliable; dependable even during trying or dangerous times 不动摇的，忠实的，可靠的

Because of unwavering devotion to its master or mistress, the golden retriever can be a *steadfast* companion. 鉴于对男女主人的一片忠诚，这只金毛猎狗绝不失为一个忠实的伙伴。

noun: **steadfastness**
adverb: **steadfastly**

►**tenacious**
/tɪˈneʃəs/
a.

• holding tight; not letting go or yielding to the opposition 紧握的；坚持的，顽强的

Margaret would not be dissuaded from her opinion; she was *tenacious* in her beliefs about *Roe v. Wade*. 玛格丽特是个很难被说服的人，她坚持自己对罗诉讼韦德案的看法。

• having the characteristic of being cohesive and adhering well to other substances 黏着力强的

Cat owners know how *tenacious* cat hair can be on their clothes and furniture. 养猫人都了解猫毛很容易粘在他们的衣服或家具上。

noun: **tenacity, tenaciousness**
adverb: **tenaciously**

►**valiant**
/ˈvæljənt/
a.

brave; full of valor and courage 英勇的，勇敢的

The *valiant* young bombardier was decorated with the Purple Heart for his heroic efforts during World War II. 这个勇敢的年轻投弹手因为在二战中的英勇表现而被授予了紫心勋章。

noun: **valiance, valiancy**
adverb: **valiantly**

►**virago**
/vəˈrego/

• a woman who is noisy, bold, or domineering 泼妇，悍妇

n.

The fisherman's wife was a real *virago*: all she did was scold and nag her husband whenever he was home. 渔夫的妻子的确是个悍妇——只要丈夫在家，她所做的一切就是去责骂和叨扰她丈夫。

- a strong, often large, courageous, and brave woman 健壮勇敢的女子

Displaying undaunted courage in her fight for decent medical care for "her" soldiers, Florence Nightingale was a true *virago* during the Crimean War. 在克里米亚战争中，弗洛伦丝·南丁格尔以大无畏的精神为战士们提供了良好的医疗服务，无愧为一名勇敢女性。

....

▶ **brash**
/bræʃ/
a.

hasty, unthinking, and impetuous; quick to act without considering the consequences 性急的，轻率的

The teen made a *brash* decision to stay out all night with his friends, but he was ultimately sorry for causing his parents such concern. 这个少年轻率地决定整晚与朋友在外玩耍，但他最终还是为自己让父母担心而深感抱歉。

adverb: **brashly**
noun: **brashness**

▶ **capricious**
/kə'prɪʃəs/
a.

impulsive, whimsical 任性的，反复无常的

In a *capricious* moment, the couple went to the next state and got married — an action they would regret for the rest of their lives. 这对男女一时冲动到另一个州结了婚，而这个决定将使他们后悔一辈子。

noun: **caprice**
adverb: **capriciously**

▶ **daring**

adjective: willing to take risks; bold and venturesome,

/'dɛrɪŋ/
a.,n.
sometimes without much sense 冒险的，勇敢的；鲁莽的

It was ***daring*** and foolish for Jerome to walk so close to the edge of the subway platform. 杰尔姆走得离地铁站台边缘很近，这既冒险又愚蠢。

noun: **courage that makes you willing to take risks** 勇气，胆量

The ***daring*** of the acrobats on the high wire was breathtaking. 杂技演员在高空钢丝绳上的大胆表演让人不得不屏住呼吸。

adverb: **daringly**

▶ **derring-do**
/'dɛrɪŋ'du/
n.
a reckless, daring, or careless action 大胆行为；鲁莽行为

The pirate's deeds of ***derring-do*** were legendary. 海盗蛮勇的行为颇具传奇色彩。

▶ **foolhardy**
/'ful,hɑrdɪ/
a.
recklessly careless; unwisely daring 莽撞的，蛮干的

Andrew wove his motorcycle in and out among the speeding cars; his ***foolhardy*** actions resulted in a bad and nearly fatal accident. 安德鲁骑着摩托车在疾驶的汽车中穿行，这种莽撞的行为导致了严重的事故，他险些丧命。

noun: **foolhardiness**

▶ **hotheaded**
/'hɑt,hɛdɪd/
a.
quick to anger; quick to act, often without regard to the consequences 易怒的；冲动的

Jerome's ***hotheaded*** response to his girlfriend's dumping him didn't surprise those who had seen his temper before. 杰尔姆在被女朋友抛弃之后的冲动表现对于那些以前见过他发脾气的人来说一点儿也不奇怪。

noun: **hotheadness**
adverb: **hotheadedly**

► **impetuous**
/ɪm'pɛtʃʊəs/
a.

impulsive and passionate, sometimes marked by violent force 冲动的，鲁莽的

Sometimes our *impetuous* decisions can prove foolhardy in the long run. 有时我们鲁莽的决定从长远来看是很愚蠢的。

adverb: **impetuously**
noun: **impetuousness**

► **impulsive**
/ɪm'pʌlsɪv/
a.

inclined to act on impulse rather than on thought; acting without thinking things through 冲动的

Impulsive behavior can get us in trouble and cause us to regret our actions. 一时的冲动会给我们带来很多麻烦，我们也会为此懊悔不已。

adverb: **impulsively**
noun: **impulse**

► **insolent**
/'ɪnsələnt/
a.

bold; arrogant; rude; rash and disrespectful 傲慢的，无礼的

The *insolent* student was caught in the act of not only imitating the teacher but also wearing the teacher's coat and hat. 这个无礼的学生被逮了个正着。他不仅模仿老师的动作，还穿上老师的外套，戴上老师的帽子。

noun: **insolence**
adverb: **insolently**

► **madcap**
/'mæd͵kæp/
a.

behaving impulsively, madly, or rashly, with little thought or consideration of consequences 冲动的，鲁莽的

The twins' *madcap* adventure left them stranded 300 miles from home with less than $5 between them. 这对双胞胎冲动的冒险行为使得他们被困在离家300英里外的地方，

口袋里的钱不足5美元。

▶ **offhanded**
/ˌɔfˈhændɪd/
a.

performed extemporaneously, without forethought or planning 即席的

Charlie gave such an *offhanded* speech that we were surprised he got a passing grade on it. 查利即席的演讲居然能及格，我们都感到惊讶。

adverb: **offhandedly**
noun: **offhandedness**

▶ **perilous**
/ˈpɛrələs/
a.

full of or involving peril or great danger 危险的，冒险的

In the book *The Lord of the Flies* the students from a private boys' school experience many *perilous* adventures when they find themselves alone and without adult supervision after their plane crashes on a deserted island. 在《蝇王》一书中，私立男子学校的学生们在飞机坠毁在一个荒岛上后，脱离了大人们的管束，也经历了许多危险事件。

adverb: **perilously**
noun: **perilousness**

▶ **rash**
/ræʃ/
a.

characterized by or resulting from ill-considered haste or boldness; reckless 鲁莽的，轻率的

Never one to make *rash* decisions, my grandfather thought over the situation for a long time before he made up his mind. 祖父从不草率行事，在做决定前反复斟酌了当时的情况。

adverb: **rashly**
noun: **rashness**

▶ **reckless**

indifferent to or disregarding of consequences; careless 轻率

/'rɛklɪs/
a.
的，不计后果的

Reckless behavior often leads to remorse and heartache later on. 轻率的行为通常会导致悔恨和心痛。

adverb: **recklessly**
noun: **recklessness**

▶**temerity**
/tə'mɛrətɪ/
n.

reckless disregard for danger or one's own safety; recklessness
鲁莽，轻率

Juana's ***temerity*** in rushing into traffic to save the runaway kitten made everyone scold her for being so careless about her own safety while praising her for what she did. 胡安娜冒失地冲进车流中救出了跑掉的小猫。大家在表扬她的同时一致指责她太不顾及自身安危了。

Sentence Completion 完成句子

Circle the word or word pair that best completes the meaning of the sentence. 圈出最符合句子含义的词或一对词。

1. Steven's _____ courage was evident during the tragedy, but Bryan, who lacked such daring, tried to hide his weakness with a swaggering _____.
   A. foolhardy/defiance
   B. insolent/gallantry
   C. dauntless/bravado
   D. steadfast/temerity
   E. tenacious/valiance

2. The frightened kitten held onto the tree limb _____, unwilling to release its grip as its _____ owner climbed a ladder to rescue it.
   A. steadfastly/plucky
   B. gallantly/defiant
   C. dauntlessly/foolhardy
   D. smugly/self-righteous
   E. tenaciously/valiant

3. During her early teens, Alexandra developed such a _____ attitude toward authority that no one wanted to be around her because she was always getting in trouble.
   A. rash
   B. stalwart
   C. defiant
   D. audacious
   E. insolent

4. Despite having had three bouts with cancer, Elsie continued to demonstrate _____ ; her courage and determination showed her to be (a) _____ , unwilling to give up or to give in.

A. fortitude/virago

B. tenacity/madcap

C. insolence/gallant

D. sanctimony/defiance

E. complaisance/valiant

5. Lewis and Clark were _____ explorers; even though they were constantly challenged by daunting circumstances, their _____ and resourcefulness kept them going.

A. steadfast/impetuousness

B. intrepid/pluck

C. valiant/insolence

D. impulsive/tenaciousness

E. audacious/bravado

Quick Matching 快速配对

Write the letter of the definition shown in the right column next to the word that matches it in the left column. 在右栏中找出与左栏单词相符的定义，将对应的字母写在单词旁。

_____ 1. insolent	A. bold and dashing
_____ 2. valiant	B. rude and arrogant
_____ 3. gallant	C. unwise and daring
_____ 4. defiant	D. valorous and courageous
_____ 5. foolhardy	E. boldly resistant

Complete the Story 完成故事

Using these words selected from this unit, fill in the blanks to complete the story. 用本单元的词汇填空，完成故事。

steadfast	rash
virago	defy
dauntless	valiantly
insolent	audacious
bravado	intrepid
daring	pluck
reckless	madcap
foolhardy	gallantly

Sir Francis Drake _____ led the fleet that defeated the Spanish Armada in 1588. Because of the _____ courage of this seafarer and his _____ ship, the *Golden Hind*, people in England greet one another today with "hello" instead of "ola." Drake truly turned Great Britain into a world power.

If we look beyond the textbook version of Sir Francis Drake, however, we discover that he was a reckless and _____ man who actually displayed more _____ than true _____. In actuality, Drake was an _____ pirate who followed many whims, and whose rude and _____ behavior had greatly displeased Queen Elizabeth I. She could be a real _____ when she became angry. In order to win back her favor, he _____ attacked the entire Spanish fleet for her. With the weather working in his favor, Drake was able to _____ the power of the Spanish Armada, and he won the sea battle in the name of his queen. Some historians scratch their

heads and wonder if Drake was truly an _____ hero or a
_____, _____ adventurer, whose _____
and _____ deeds just happened to go the right way.

ANSWERS 答案

Sentence Completion 完成句子： 1-C, 2-E, 3-C, 4-A, 5-B

Quick Matching 快速配对： 1-B, 2-D, 3-A, 4-E, 5-C

Complete the Story 完成故事： valiantly, dauntless, steadfast, foolhardy, bravado, pluck, audacious, insolent, virago, gallantly, defy, intrepid, daring, madcap, rash, reckless (Last two are interchangeable.)

One Size Does *Not* Fit All
一种规格不可能处处合适

有时候小的（*small*）、微小的（*tiny*）、大的（*large, big*）这样的词不足以准确地描述一幅图景。下面有许多描写尺寸、数量和重要程度的词，你应该可以找到一个合适的词来表达你的意思。同时你也会发现，这些词中有不少是近义词。有些词略有区别，但有些词意思基本相同。

dearth	minuscule	pittance
diminutive	minute	scant
infinitesimal	mite	scintilla
insignificant	negligible	trifling
Lilliputian	paucity	trivial
meager	petty	

....

ample	humongous	plethora
behemoth	immeasurable	prodigious
Brobdingnagian	incalculable	statuesque
colossal	infinite	surfeit
copious	mammoth	titanic
gargantuan	monumental	

► **dearth**
/dɝθ/

n.

a scarcity or lack of supply 缺乏，短缺

During World War II there was a *dearth* of silk available for women's stockings because the military needed the silk for making parachutes. 二战期间可用来制作女士长袜的蚕丝很短缺，因为军队需要用蚕丝做降落伞。

► **diminutive**
/dəˈmɪnjətɪv/

a.

very small; tiny (*Diminutive* is occasionally used as a noun. It refers to anything that is small or the name given to suffixes on words that indicate smallness. For example, the suffix *let* is a diminutive. When it is added to a noun, it indicates a smaller version of that noun, such as a *booklet* or *starlet*.) 很小的，极小的（该词偶尔也作名词用。它指任何小的事物，或者表示"小"的意思的后缀。例如后缀let就是一个diminutive，加在名词后面时则表示为该名词的更小版本，比如：booklet或starlet。）

Tinkerbell is the *diminutive* fairy in the children's story *Peter Pan*. 小叮当是童话故事《彼得·潘》中的一个小仙女。

adverb: **diminutively**
noun: **diminutiveness**

► **infinitesimal**
/ˌɪnfɪnəˈtɛsəml̩/

a.

immeasurably or incalculably small 极微小的

At one time scientists thought they would never be able to study the *infinitesimal* nucleus of the atom, but, with advanced technology, this study is commonplace. 科学家们曾经认为不可能对原子内的极其微小的原子核进行研究，但随着技术的发展，这项研究就很普遍了。

adverb: **infinitesimally**

► **insignificant** • of little importance or power 不重要的
/ˌɪnsɪgˈnɪfəkənt/

a.

Everyday, routine, personal problems seem *insignificant* when compared to the problems of drought, famine, or war. 日常的例行的私人问题与干旱、饥荒或战争等问题相比就显得无足轻重了。

• small and not important 微不足道的

After the accident, the dent in the car door was *insignificant* compared to the damage the other car suffered. 事故发生后，这辆汽车车门上的凹痕与另一辆车的受损情况相比是不值一提的。

adverb: **insignificantly**
noun: **insignificance**

▶ **Lilliputian**
/ˌlɪləˈpjuʃən/
n., a.

noun: a very tiny person or thing (This word is taken from Jonathan Swift's *Gulliver's Travels*. In this book the *Lilliputians* are very tiny people who live in the land of Lilliput, which is where Gulliver experienced his first adventure.) 极小的人或物（该词来源于乔纳森·斯威夫特的小说《格列佛游记》。该书中Lilliputians指居住在Lilliput地的小人儿们，该地是格列佛冒险的第一站。）

When Michael Jordan visits the children's wards in hospitals, he is like a giant among the adoring and appreciative *Lilliputians*. 当迈克尔·乔丹造访医院里的儿童病房时，他就像个巨人站在崇拜和景仰他的小人儿国国民面前。

adjective:

• small or trivial in size 微小的

The young couple found a *lilliputian* cottage that suited their needs for a temporary home. 这对年轻夫妇找到了一间小农舍作为临时居所。

• not important, petty 微不足道的，不重要的

The question was *lilliputian* in light of the seriousness of the situation. 在严峻的情势下，这个问题显得很微不足道。

▶ **meager**
/'migɚ/
a.

• scarce in quantity or extent; in short supply 数量少的，短缺的

After two weeks of rough camping in the hot, humid, mosquito-infested Minnesota Boundary Waters, good humor and food were in *meager* supply while flaring tempers were plentiful. 在潮湿闷热且蚊子大群出没的明尼苏达边境水域旁艰难宿营两周后，幽默感和食物一样成了短缺品，不乏的是人们越来越暴躁的脾气。

• deficient in richness or fertility 贫瘠的

Because the soil was so *meager*, the crops yielded very little harvest. 由于土壤十分贫瘠，因此庄稼的收成很不好。

adverb: **meagerly**
noun: **meagerness**

▶ **minuscule**
/mɪ'nʌskjul/
(sometimes spelled **miniscule**)
/'mɪnɪskjul/
a., n.

adjective: **extremely tiny; very small** 极小的

When cooking with hot Thai dragon peppers, the chef must use *minuscule* amounts, or the peppers will overpower all other flavors of the dish being prepared. 做菜时若要加入泰国龙胡椒，厨师只能添加极少的量，否则胡椒的味道将盖过其他食材的味道。

noun:

• small, ancient, cursive script 草写小字

Some of the *minuscules* in the ancient manuscript were so faded that the translators were unable to transcribe the entire text. 古时遗存的手稿中有些草写小字褪色严重，翻译人员很难将原文完整地抄写下来。

- lowercase letters 小写字母

An old-fashioned term for lowercase letters is *minuscule*. "minuscule" 是 "lowercase letter" 的一种过时的表达方式。

▶ **minute**
/məˈnjuːt/
a.

- exceptionally small or insignificant 极小的；不重要的

The hardly visible dent in the car door seemed *minute* to me, but the car's owner was displeased nevertheless. 汽车门上很难发现的小凹痕对我来说完全可以忽略，但车主却非常不满。

- characterized by precise and close scrutiny 细致入微的

The drill sergeant held a *minute* inspection of the recruits' quarters, looking for a shoe unpolished or blanket not taut. 负责训练的警官很仔细地搜寻了新兵的宿舍，检查鞋子是否光亮以及毯子是否整洁。

adverb: **minutely**

▶ **mite**
/maɪt/
n.

- a very small sum of money 很少的钱

Widow's mite is a biblical reference to a poor widow whose small donation meant more to her than much larger sums from those who could easily manage to contribute. **Widow's mite**这一典故出自《圣经》，讲的是一个穷寡妇捐的很小一笔钱比那些有钱人捐的一大笔钱更有价值。

- a very small creature or object 小生物；小物品

The orphan child was a *mite* — undersized because of her

poor care. 这个孤儿看上去很瘦小，她因缺乏照料而发育不良。

The tiny premature infant seemed like a *mite* next to the 9-pound baby in the next crib. 在这个9磅重宝宝的床旁边，这个小小的早产儿看起来像只小虫。

▶ **negligible**
/'nɛglədʒəbl/
a.

not considered important enough to be worth bothering about; insignificant 可以忽视的，微不足道的

When I receive a *negligible* amount in change from a restaurant bill, I toss the money into the dish by the cash register. 在餐馆结完账后，我把找我的很少一点儿钱扔进了收款台旁的盘子里。

noun: **negligibility**
adverb: **negligibly**

▶ **paucity**
/'pɔsətɪ/
n.

• smallness of number 少量

The county officials were disappointed when only a *paucity* of voters turned out for the election. 只有很少人来为选举投票，县里的官员们很失望。

• scarcity of amount 贫乏，缺乏

During the drought, there was such a *paucity* of water that the local swimming pools had to close down. 干旱时节，严重缺水使得当地的游泳池不得不关闭。

▶ **petty**
/'pɛtɪ/
a.

• trivial; of little importance 琐碎的；不重要的

Because she had much on her mind while planning her wedding, the bride-to-be left the *petty* details to be taken care of by others. 由于即将成为新娘的她要为筹备婚礼操很多心，因此她把一些琐碎的细节交给他人代办了。

• narrow-minded; shortsighted 心胸狭窄的；目光短浅的

Sandra was so *petty* that she overlooked the big picture because she was so concerned about trivialities. 桑德拉目光短浅，只注重细节而忽略了对全局的把握。

• mean and grudging 记仇的

The old woman was so *petty* that she held a grudge for years over some minor insult. 这个老妇女很记仇，对曾经受过的小小的侮辱，她多年以来一直怀恨在心。

adverb: **pettily**
noun: **pettiness**

▶**pittance**
/ˈpɪtn̩s/
n.

a very small amount, often referring to an unusually meager amount of money 微薄的薪酬

After dropping out of college, the young man could not find employment and had to settle for earning a *pittance* from a job he found working in a kiosk at the mall. 这个年轻人大学辍学后找不到工作，只能靠在商场的小摊位上打工来挣得微薄的收入。

▶**scant**
/skænt/
a., v.

adjective: barely sufficient; falling short of a necessary amount; inadequately supplied 不足的，缺乏的

Because of threatening thunderstorms, only a *scant* crowd gathered for the band concert in the park. 由于雷阵雨将要来临，到公园来参加音乐会的人很稀少。

verb: To shortchange or deal with something inadequately or neglectfully 削减，减少

Because of her demanding work hours as a lawyer on her

way up in the firm, Susan *scanted* on quality time with her children. 由于律师所对律师的工作时间有很严格的要求，苏珊削减了与孩子待在一起的时间。

adverb: **scantily**
noun: **scantiness**

►**scintilla**
/sɪn'tɪlə/
n.

a minute amount; barely a suggestion; just an inkling or a spark 一点点

For a brief moment, Carlos had a *scintilla* of hope that he would not get lost in the blizzard. 一瞬间卡洛斯有了一丝希望，认为自己也许不会在暴风雪中迷失方向。

►**trifling**
/'traɪflɪŋ/
a.

of trivial or nonsensical importance; not important and easily dismissed 微不足道的，不重要的

Heidi's *trifling* plan was so impossible to carry out that everyone dismissed it immediately. 海迪小小的计划根本行不通，大家很快就否决了他的提议。

noun: **trifle**

►**trivial**
/'trɪvɪəl/
a.

of little significance or importance; concerned with trivia or inconsequential information; commonplace 琐碎的；没有意义的；普通的

Although the research assignment was supposed to get students to find new and unusual information, Alfred could find only *trivial* facts and unimportant details. 尽管课题研究作业在于让学生发现新的不寻常的信息，艾尔弗雷德只找到了一些琐碎的事实和一些无足轻重的细节。

adverb: **trivially**
noun: **triviality**

▶ **ample**
/ˈæmpl̩/
a.

of a large or great size; fully sufficient, even more than enough 尺寸大的；充足的，充裕的

I remember my grandmother as a large woman with an *ample* lap for me to sit on. 我记得祖母很高大，我总坐在她宽宽的膝盖上。

adverb: **amply**
noun: **ampleness**

▶ **behemoth**
/bɪˈhiːmɑθ/
n.

something that is enormous in size and/or power 庞然大物

The super jet was a *behemoth* flying from Los Angeles to Hong Kong and carrying nearly 300 passengers. 这架从洛杉矶飞往香港的超级喷气式飞机是个庞然大物，容纳了将近300名旅客。

▶ **Brobding-**
nagian
/brɑbdɪŋ-
ˈnægɪən/
a.

immense or enormous (The word comes from Jonathan Swift's *Gulliver's Travels*. In his second adventure, Gulliver finds himself in Brobdingnag, the land of the giants.) 巨大的（该词来源于乔纳森·斯威夫特的小说《格列佛游记》。在格列佛第二次的探险旅程中，他发现自己来到了Brobdingnag，一个巨人王国。）

A giant cherry on an enormous spoon is a famous Minneapolis, Minnesota, sculpture of *Brobdingnagian* proportions. 一颗巨大的樱桃置于一把巨大的汤勺上，这是位于明尼苏达州明尼阿波利斯市著名的巨型雕塑。

▶ **colossal**
/kəˈlɑsl̩/
a.

so enormous or gigantic that it seems to defy belief 巨大的，庞大的

Until one actually sees the huge stones at Stonehenge, England, a person cannot appreciate what a *colossal* undertaking it must have been. 若不是亲眼看到英国史前的巨石阵，人们无论如何也无法想象它到底有多巨大。

► **copious**
/'kopɪəs/
a.

containing or yielding plenty; bountiful in amount or manner 丰富的，大量的

Afraid she might miss something in the biology lecture, Arlene not only took *copious* notes, but she also brought her tape recorder to class. 担心错过生物课上的要点，阿琳不仅做了大量的笔记，还把录音机带到了教室。

adverb: **copiously**
noun: **copiousness**

► **gargantuan**
/gɑr'gæntʃʊən/
a.

of enormous size, quantity, or volume or capacity 巨大的，庞大的，大量的

The grounds of mansion were enormous, and Marty thought he would never get the *gargantuan* lawn mowed and its edges trimmed. 大楼前面的草地宽阔之极，以至于马蒂认为他无法完成割草和修剪的任务。

► **humongous**
/hju'mɑŋgəs/
(sometimes spelled **humungous**)
/hju'mʌŋgəs/
a.

gigantic or extremely oversized 庞大的

After the two-hour practice, we were so hungry that the four of us devoured a *humongous* pizza and at least five liters of Pepsi. 两个小时的训练让我们四个人饥饿难耐，共消灭了一个巨型比萨和至少五升百事可乐。

► **immeasurable**
/ɪ'mɛʒərəbl̩/
a.

so vast or limitless in size that measurement is not possible 大得无法计量的

The young couple felt *immeasurable* love for their newborn baby. 这对年轻夫妇对他们刚出生的宝宝有着无尽的疼爱。

adverb: **immeasurably**
noun: **immeasurability**

▶ **incalculable** impossible or too great to be calculated or resolved 无法计
/ɪnˈkælkjələbl̩/ 算的，数不清的
a.

> Because the storm caused *incalculable* damage to the small town, insurance representatives were flown in from everywhere. 暴风雨使小镇遭受了不可估量的损失，各地的保险代理人都纷纷赶来。

> adverb: **incalculably**
> noun: **incalculability**

▶ **infinite** immeasurably great or large; having no limits or boundaries
/ˈɪnfənɪt/ 无穷大的；无限的，无边的
a.

> Despite having to deal with a class of 30 squirming, energetic kindergartners, the teacher displayed *infinite* patience. 尽管要照看班上30个躁动而精力充沛的小孩，这个幼儿园老师仍旧表现出了极大的耐心。

> noun: **infinity**
> adv: **infinitely**

▶ **mammoth** noun:
/ˈmæməθ/
n., a.
> • a great, hairy, prehistoric elephantlike creature 猛犸，毛象

> Archeologists discovered the well-preserved remains of a prehistoric *mammoth*. 考古学家发现了一具保存完好的史前猛犸的遗骸。

> • anything of unusual size 庞然大物

> adjective: enormous; of great or unusual size or proportions 庞大的，巨大的

Driving the **mammoth** Humvee was a much different experience from driving a Miata. 开这辆巨型的悍马车与开一辆马自达的感觉是完全不同的。

▶**monumental** • resembling a monument 丰碑式的；非凡的
/ˌmɑnjəˈmɛntl̩/

a.　　The Egyptian Pharaoh's **monumental** bearing was impressive to his minions. 这位埃及法老威严的气质给他的臣民留下了极深的印象。

• exceptionally large, sturdy, or enduring 巨大的；不朽的

When the teacher assigned the research paper, it seemed like a **monumental** undertaking that I would never be able to complete. 老师布置的研究论文对我而言就像一项永远难以完成的宏伟工程。

adverb: **monumentally**

▶**plethora**　　an excessive amount; a surplus 过剩，剩余
/ˈplɛθərə/

n.　　Because the office assistant thought the boss wanted 12 dozen folders instead of only 12 folders, we had a **plethora** of blue and red folders at our disposal. 因为办公室助理误认为老板需要12打文件夹而不是仅仅12个文件夹，于是我们就有了大量剩余的蓝色和红色文件夹。

▶**prodigious** • excessively great in size, force, or content 巨大的，庞大的
/prəˈdɪdʒəs/

a.　　The hurricane caused such **prodigious** rain and wind that many houses were severely damaged. 飓风引发了强降雨和大风，许多房屋被严重损毁了。

• exceptionally talented 才华出众的
Lindsay was such a **prodigious** student that she was in two advanced placement classes, the dance squad and the speech

team. 林赛是个才华出众的学生，她参加了两个高级别的团队：舞蹈队和辩论队。

adverb: **prodigiously**
noun: **prodigiousness**

▶**statuesque**
/ˌstætʃʊˈɛsk/
a.

- unusually large or outstanding in carriage and/or demeanor 端庄优美的

The *statuesque* news anchor drew everyone's attention — men and women alike. 这个端庄优美的新闻主播吸引了每个人的眼球，无论男女。

▶**surfeit**
/ˈsɜˑfɪt/
n., v.

noun:

- overindulgence, as in food or drink 饮食过度
- an excessive amount 过量

The United States is often looked upon as a country of overindulged people who have a *surfeit* of material goods at their disposal. 美国经常被贬低为一个暴饮暴食的国度，在这里人们拥有着过量的物质生活用品。

verb: to feed or supply to excess, even to the point of disgust 使厌腻；使（饮食等）过量；过多地供给

Many successful farmers were able to *surfeit* some of their bumper crops to the countries that had been devastated by the hurricane. 许多成功的农民都能向那些因飓风而遭受严重损失的国家大量提供他们收获的粮食。

▶**titanic**
/taɪˈtænɪk/
a.

- of or relating to something awesome or great in size or scope 巨大的，极大的

In September 1989, Hurricane Hugo was a storm of such *titanic* proportions that large areas of South Carolina were completely devastated by its high winds and torrential rains, at least 26 people died, and parts of the Charleston area landscape were changed forever. **1989年9月，飓风"雨果"浩浩荡荡地席卷了南卡罗来纳州大部分地区，强风劲雨导致至少26人死亡，并且查尔斯顿部分地区的地貌被永久地改变了。**

Sentence Completion 完成句子

Circle the word or word pair that best completes the meaning of the sentence. 圈出最符合句子含义的词或一对词。

1. Some news stations report such _____ information that many viewers consider their stories as _____ and not worth their attention.
   A. diminutive/infinitesimal
   B. insignificant/trivial
   C. minute/petty
   D. ample/trifling
   E. meager/incalculable

2. Because of ideal weather conditions last year, Iowa had a _____ of corn, so the state was able to export some of its harvest.
   A. dearth
   B. paucity
   C. monument
   D. surfeit
   E. scintilla

3. The information Sandy found in the reference book was so _____ that she didn't even bother to take any notes.
   A. diminutive
   B. petty
   C. immeasurable
   D. scant
   E. incalculable

4. In the next reference, however, Sandy discovered a
   _____ of information, so she took _____ notes
   on her topic.
   A. ampleness/minute
   B. dearth/incalculable
   C. paucity/immeasurable
   D. mammoth/surfeit
   E. plethora/copious

5. Despite some _____ complaints among the 300
   passengers, the _____ overseas jet made good time
   between New York and London.
   A. petty/colossal
   B. paucity/monumental
   C. modicum/statuesque
   D. scintilla/prodigious
   E. infinitesimal/ample

Quick Matching 快速配对

*Write the letter of the definition shown in the right column next
to the word that matches it in the left column.* 在右栏中找出与
左栏单词相符的定义，将对应的字母写在单词旁。

_____ 1. pittance	A.	fully sufficient; more than enough
_____ 2. ample	B.	suggestive of a monument
_____ 3. Brobdingnagian	C.	little money
_____ 4. statuesque	D.	incalculably small
_____ 5. infinitesimal	E.	immense or enormous

Complete the Story 完成故事

Using these words selected from this unit, fill in the blanks to complete the story. 用本单元的词汇填空，完成故事。

infinite	prodigious
colossal	gargantuan
copious	incalculable
plethora	diminutive
minute	monumental
scintilla	minuscule
immeasurable	humongous
insignificant	

From its often _____ depths and the _____ number of creatures living in the water or on its beaches, the ocean provides us with a _____ of contrasting sizes. _____ starfish may be no bigger than the nail on your little finger, but other starfish species can be the size of an extra-large pizza. _____ humpback whales dine on _____ amounts of _____, nearly invisible plankton. Humpback infants, however, could never be called _____ newborns. These youngsters weigh in at a _____ 1,500-2,000 lb at birth! _____ coral reefs are also living creatures within the ocean. They are slow-growing, however, showing barely a _____ of change during the course of a year. The variety of fish species living in the oceans and seas is _____. The smallest nurse shark may be a scant 10 inches long, and the infamous great white shark, whose _____ strength and menace were made famous by the movie *Jaws*. Finally, we cannot overlook the crab. The most _____ of this species is the soldier crab, measuring a mere 15 millimeters, while the _____ giant crab can measure over 400 millimeters. Creatures great and small can be found in the ocean.

ANSWERS 答案
Sentence Completion 完成句子：1-B, 2-D, 3-D, 4-E, 5-A
Quick Matching 快速配对：1-C, 2-A, 3-E, 4-B, 5-D
Complete the Story 完成故事：immeasurable, incalculable, plethora, Diminutive, Gargantuan, copious, minuscule, minute, colossal, Monumental, scintilla, infinite, prodigious, insignificant, humongous

Review 3 复习 3

These sentences include words from the previous five units. 下列句子需要使用前面五个单元的词汇。

Sentence Completion 完成句子

Circle the word pair that best completes the meaning of the sentence. 圈出最符合句子含义的一对词。

1. The poor, struggling college student found that his scholarship money gave him only a _____ to live on, so he had to find a job in order to have enough food.
   A. pittance
   B. immeasurability
   C. surfeit
   D. mammoth
   E. scintilla

2. Even though the generous congressman had been _____ in his support of the arts and charities, the press did not hesitate to _____ him when his name was linked to a local scandal in his home state.
   A. admirable/eulogize
   B. penurious/disparage
   C. laudable/extol
   D. selfless/abominate
   E. magnanimous/excoriate

3. The performer became so impressed with herself that her
   _____ attitude caused her fans to dislike her for her
   _____ behavior.
   A. frugal/audacious
   B. reproachful/creditable
   C. haughty/reprehensible
   D. egocentric/estimable
   E. admonitory/reckless

4. The crystal figurine was _____, despite the
   _____ value that the insurance company had placed
   upon it.
   A. infinitesimal/meager
   B. diminutive/colossal
   C. copious/infinite
   D. incalculable/insignificant
   E. a pittance/negligible

5. Although Louis was _____ and fun to be around,
   his high spirits often led to _____ behavior that
   sometimes got him in trouble.
   A. audacious/priggish
   B. convivial/impetuous
   C. admiral/selfless
   D. intrepid/deplorable
   E. amiable/creditable

6. Pamela is a quiet girl whose _____ is often mistaken for _____ by people who don't make the effort to get to know her.

A. reticence/aloofness
B. steadfastness/parsimony
C. geniality/insolence
D. tenacity/providence
E. self-righteousness/altruism

7. Bruce had always been a poor loser, so when the referee called a foul, instead of reacting in a sportsmanlike, _____ manner, he let his _____ nature provoke him into arguing with the referee.

A. openhanded/deplorable
B. gallant/smug
C. penurious/madcap
D. laudable/hotheaded
E. benevolent/resolute

ANSWERS 答案
1-A, 2-E, 3-C, 4-B, 5-B, 6-A, 7-D

Index

索 引

Essential SAT words have bold locators.

Pronunciation Table K.K.音标和IPA对照表

Consonants 辅音

K.K.		KEY WORD 例词
p	p	**pen**
b	b	**back**
t	t	**ten**
d	d	**day**
k	k	**key**
g	g	**get**
f	f	**fat**
v	v	**view**
θ	θ	**thing**
ð	ð	**then**
s	s	**soon**
z	z	**zero**
ʃ	ʃ	**ship**
ʒ	ʒ	**pleasure**
h	h	**hot**
x	x	**loch**
tʃ	tʃ	**cheer**
dʒ	dʒ	**jump**
m	m	**sum**
n	n	**sun**
ṇ	n	**adjacent**
ŋ	ŋ	**sung**
w	w	**wet**
l	l	**let**
ḷ	l	**stable**
r	r	**red**
j	j	**yet**

Vowels 元音

	K.K.	IPA	KEY WORD 例词
short 短元音	ɪ	ɪ	**bit**
	ɛ	e	**bed**
	æ	æ	**cat**
	ɑ	ɒ	**pot**
	ʌ	ʌ	**but**
	ʊ	ʊ	**put**
	ʊ	u	**actuality**
	ə	ə	**about**
	ɪ	i	**happy**
long 长元音	i	iː	**sheep**
	ɑ	ɑː	**father**
	ɔ	ɔː	**talk**
	ɔr	ɔː	**four**
	u	uː	**boot**
	ɝ	ɜː	**bird**
diphthongs 双元音	e	eɪ	**make**
	aɪ	aɪ	**lie**
	ɔɪ	ɔɪ	**boy**
	o	əʊ	**note**
	aʊ	aʊ	**now**
	ɪr	ɪə	**rear**
	ɪə	eɪ	**India**
	ɛr	eə	**hair**
	ʊr	ʊə	**sure**
	ʊə	uə	**actual**
	jɚ	iə	**peculiar**

注：本书以K.K.音标标示美国音。